EXPANDING HORIZONS IN SOCIAL WORK AND ALLIED PROFESSIONS

**CHILDREN AND YOUNG PEOPLE WHO SEXUALLY ABUSE OTHERS:
POLICY AND PRACTICE DEVELOPMENTS SINCE THE EARLY 1990s**

Helen Masson

Series Editors: Brian Littlechild and Karen Lyons

BASW website: http://www.basw.co.uk

Published by
VENTURE PRESS
16 Kent Street
Birmingham
B5 6RD

British Library Cataloguing-in-Publication Data
A catalogue record for this book is available from the British Library

ISBN   1 86178 067 2 (paperback)

Cover design by:
Western Arts
21b Highgate Close
London
N6 4SD

Printed in Great Britain

CONTENTS

PAGE

CONTENTS

This monograph comprises, firstly, an overview of literature and research into children and young people who sexually abuse others covering how this group appears to have emerged as a problem during the 1990s; incidence and prevalence issues; current knowledge about the characteristics of young sexual abusers; an outline and critique of prevailing treatment approaches; and consideration of the issue of recidivism. The monograph then outlines the findings from empirical research conducted by the author during the middle to late 1990s into the state of policy and practice developments in relation to young sexual abusers in England. The findings from the literature overview and the research are then analysed within broader conceptual frameworks before, finally, the monograph discusses the impact of recent national policy and legislative developments in both child welfare/protection and youth crime on this area of work, with some suggestions for the implications for policy and practice issues at the local level.

The monograph focuses particularly on developments in England, rather than in the UK as a whole. Further research is underway in order to gain equivalent information about developments in Northern Ireland, Scotland and Wales (Hackett, Masson and Philips, in progress).

CHAPTER 1
THE EMERGENCE OF THE PROBLEM OF CHILDREN AND YOUNG PEOPLE WHO SEXUALLY ABUSE

The regulation of sexual relationships between adults and between adults and children through folklore, informal sanctions, religious mores and laws and criminal legislation has been a feature of societies for centuries, with attitudes changing over time about the acceptability of various forms of sexual contact (Kilpatrick, 1992). Only in the case of incest would there appear to have been some consensus over the centuries, with such intra-familial sexual behaviour being the subject of taboos in most societies throughout history for a variety of reasons, including concerns about undermining family stability and good order, weakening the genetic stock and, more recently, because it has been perceived as abusive of children. Kilpatrick (1992) and others (see, for example, Corby 1998) provide interesting and detailed overviews of the regulation of sexuality from antiquity to the twentieth century, but for the purposes of this outline, attention will be focused on developments in relation to conceptualisations about child sexual abuse and to concerns about sex offenders since the late nineteenth century in the UK.

CHILD SEXUAL ABUSE

Focusing on child sexual abuse, Corby (2000) has argued that modern concerns about the sexual treatment of children can be traced back to the late nineteenth century, although initially the focus was on extra-familial abuse such as child prostitution. However by the turn of the century attention was also being paid to intra-familial sexual abuse, as a result of the work of organisations such as the NSPCC and in 1908 the Incest Act was passed. However prosecutions for incest remained low for many decades, until the mid 1980s, and for much of the first half of the twentieth century, on the basis of Freudian ideas about the nature of sexuality and his attribution of childhood sexual issues to the imagination of the unconscious mind (Freud, 1978, translated from original work published in 1905), accounts of sexual victimisation or sexual offending were often seen as fantasies symptomatic of intra-psychic conflicts and the realities and extent of child sexual abuse were denied (Ryan and Lane, 1991).

However from the mid 1960s onwards public and professional concerns about child abuse in general and about child sexual abuse in particular have spiralled and have been associated with ever more detailed legislative and organisational arrangements for the protection of children from such abuse. A detailed social constructionist analysis of such developments is not possible here and has been thoroughly explored elsewhere (e.g. Parton, 1985; 1991) but it would appear that a number of factors and pressure groups were associated with the emerging discourse. In respect of concerns and responses to child sexual abuse specifically, Corby (1998) cites various influences, in the USA and in the UK, which came together to put intra and extra-familial child sexual abuse firmly on the public agenda:

- the work of child protectionists such as Kempe and his colleagues in relation to the 'battered baby syndrome' (see, for example, Kempe et al, 1962) and Finkelhor (1979) in relation to sexually victimised children;
- early perspectives on the dynamics of intra-familial child sexual abuse (and father-daughter incest in particular) being promulgated by clinicians such as Giaretto (1981), Furniss (1983), Trepper and Barrett (1986) and Bentovim et al (1988), although these were by no means uncontested, with feminists and others criticising the tendency of

these perspectives to take the responsibility for the abuse off fathers and to blame what were perceived as colluding mothers (see, for example, Ward, 1984; Nelson, 1987; Masson and O'Byrne, 1990);

● the work of psychologists and psychiatrists into adult sexual abusers which will be elaborated on shortly;

● feminist analyses of male violence which was then and is still perceived as rooted in the unequal power relationships between men and women at both a personal and structural level, that is, in the patriarchal nature of society, resulting in the sexual exploitation and abuse of adult women and female children, both within and outside the family (see, for example, MacKinnon, 1982; Kelly, 1987 and Parton, 1990).

Thus a consensus began to emerge that child sexual abuse, both within and outside the family, was relatively common, that intra-familial sexual abuse occurred in families in all socio-economic groups, that children's stories about such abuse should be believed and that sexual abuse of children was morally wrong, was a serious crime and resulted in serious socio-emotional short and long term effects.

Corby (1998) provides an account of how these ideas impacted on professional practice in the UK, driven largely, in the early to mid 1980s, by 'informed' child protectionists in local areas and pressure from female sexual abuse survivors. Before the Cleveland intra-familial child sexual abuse crisis (HMSO, 1988), such developments in practice, which were pursued under the umbrella of existing child protection arrangements for dealing with physical abuse and neglect, were patchy across the country and led by front-line practitioners in various professions. However, as Corby comments:

Events in 1987 at Cleveland ensured government intervention and a more concerted effort to develop a top-led strategy in respect of child sexual abuse.(Corby, 1998: p. 33)

Thus, a more co-ordinated, procedurally led and strategic inter-agency approach to child sexual abuse began to emerge as a result of governmental guidance (DoH, 1988a, 1991) and changes implemented within successive pieces of criminal justice legislation (in 1988, 1991 and 1994) aimed, on the one hand, at reducing the possibility of secondary abuse of children (and their carers) resulting from what were perceived to be over-zealous and precipitate interventions in families (as claimed in the Cleveland Report) whilst, on the other hand, maintaining a focus on the seriousness of actual child sexual abuse and the need to prosecute sex offenders.

THE DEVELOPMENT OF RESEARCH AND INTERVENTIONS WITH ADULT SEX OFFENDERS

Although it would seem that modern day society is in the grip of an unprecedented and intense moral panic (Cohen, 1973) about (adult) sex offenders, and paedophiles in particular, in fact Sampson (1994) argues convincingly that panics about sexual crime are nothing new. He cites various examples from the fifteenth century onwards which illustrate that the public has regularly been exercised, if not obsessed, with notions that they, or their children, are at risk of sexual assault. He also suggests, as Cohen (1973) and Richards (1990) have done, that such sexual deviants are often a convenient scapegoat when the social order is perceived to be under threat in various ways. Nevertheless, although sex offenders may be scapegoated in this fashion, it is also certainly the case that sexual assault exists and that the suffering caused to the victims of such assaults, whether they be adults or children, should not be underestimated (Glaser and Frosh, 1988; Morrison et al, 1994; Ryan and Lane, 1997).

In the United Kingdom, as awareness of what is referred to as child sexual abuse increased during the 1980s, so there was a rise in the number of such cases being dealt with by those agencies seen as having a primary task in child protection: social services departments, the NSPCC and primary health professionals. Thus, Corby (1993) charted the rapid growth in the number of children being registered under DoH categories because of sexual abuse, rising from less than 1 per cent of total registrations in 1978 to almost 9 per cent in 1984 and to 25 per cent in 1986.

The problem for these 'child protection' agencies rapidly became one of finding a way off the treadmill of dealing with the consequences of child sexual abuse without dealing with the immediate cause, i.e., adult men, inside and outside the family, who had already abused children and who were judged as likely to do so again if their offending behaviour was not addressed. For agencies with a focus on the alleged abuser, such as probation, prison, police, psychological and psychiatric services, the issue became one of providing effective interventions for what was perceived to be singularly persistent and damaging behaviour in a context where the efforts of such agencies did not seem to be supported by the courts or existing treatment facilities. As Morrison comments, whilst there was an explosion of sexual abuse registrations during the mid 1980s:

In the same period, prosecutions for sexual offences rose by only 17 per cent (Home Office, 1989). In other words ... the criminal justice system appeared to be ineffective in identifying and controlling the offenders. Apart from a very limited amount of treatment being provided in NHS settings, services to sex offenders were almost non-existent until the later part of the 1980's. (Morrison et al, 1994: p. 26)

Nevertheless, research into the characteristics of child molesters and other sexual offenders (both intra- and extra- familial), and associated theorising about the causes of their behaviour and possible intervention approaches, was gathering momentum from the late 1970s onwards, particularly in North America (see, for example, Groth, 1979, Gibbens et al, 1981, Baxter et al, 1984, Prentky et al, 1989 and Knight and Prentky, 1990). As is discussed later in this overview, much of this research and theorising was being (and still is) conducted by forensic and clinical psychologists and psychiatrists, those professionals most likely to be involved in the assessment and treatment of adult sex offenders. This dominance has resulted in the development of certain preferred models of understanding and intervention, with models derived from work with adult sex offenders being adopted, with adaptations, for use in work with young sexual abusers. A critique of these current approaches is provided later in this overview, for the moment the focus is on knowledge generated about adult sex offenders from studies conducted since the late 1970s.

Fisher (1994) argues that a study of 561 non-incarcerated sex offenders by Abel and his colleagues (Abel et al, 1987):

represented a watershed in the knowledge base about sex offenders, because of the huge amount of previously unknown information revealed and served to dispel some previously held ideas and stereotypes. (Fisher, 1994: p. 6)

The subjects in this study were aged between 13 and 76 years, with an average age of 31.5 years. Most were moderately educated, half were in stable relationships and 65 per cent were fully employed. They were representative of the ethnic groups in the general population and came from all socio-economic groupings. A significant proportion of the sample (24 per cent of those who had assaulted females and 60 per cent of those who had assaulted males) reported that they were themselves abused as children (a finding supported by other studies such as those referred to above).

The 561 sex offenders in the study self-reported an unexpectedly large amount of offending (291,737 paraphilic acts), with the majority of individuals offending against a few victims occasionally, and a minority accounting for substantial numbers of victims and offences. Of particular interest was the finding there was a high level of cross-over between sexually deviant behaviours – 23 per cent of the subjects offended against both family and non-family victims. Previously it had been assumed that offenders only indulged in one kind of offence and with one kind of victim, with a distinction typically drawn between intra-familial and extra-familial sexual offending.

Subsequent studies (for example, Bradford et al, 1988; Kelly et al, 1991) have confirmed that the majority of child molesters sexually assault children they know, Grubin (1998) reporting that most studies find this to be the case at least three quarters of the time, with up to 80per cent of offences taking place in either the home of the offender or the home of the victim. In other respects, such as criminal background, their sexual arousal patterns, social functioning and their risk of re-offending, child molesters and other sex offenders emerge as a heterogeneous group, although various studies have tried to develop sub classifications or typologies based on, for example, type of offence and the characteristics of victims targeted (Conte, 1985, Lanyon, 1986 and Knight and Prentky, 1990).

By the late 1980s a slowly increasing number of treatment projects for adult sex offenders were being developed locally, often involving professionals working jointly across child protection and offender focused agencies and predominantly based on group work programmes (Barker and Morgan, 1993). Such projects were informed by the work of various prominent North American researchers and clinicians (see the studies cited above, as well as Finkelhor, 1984 and Wolf, 1984 to whom reference will be made later in this overview). Their approaches were being promulgated through national conferences and training events led by a few well known figures in this country. These included, for example, Ray Wyre, an ex prison officer, who was then running the Gracewell Clinic, a private clinic in the Midlands specialising in the treatment of male, adult sex offenders. Even then, however, the work that was being done with adult male sex offenders was largely being driven by a small number of dedicated and enthusiastic front-line professionals, or reticulists as Hallett and Birchall (1992) would describe them, rather than as a result of clearly thought out top-down policies and mandates, an impression supported by Morrison's later analysis (Morrison et al, 1994). However, since the early 1990s, partly as a result of even more heightened public concern about adult sex offenders and paedophiles especially and as a result of developing responses to child sexual abuse which have been outlined previously, provision for the treatment of adult sex offenders has, over the last decade, become more mandated and available, often being centred on probation and prison services (HM Inspectorate of Probation, 1998).

INDICATIONS OF OFFICIAL CONCERN ABOUT CHILDREN AND YOUNG PEOPLE WHO SEXUALLY ABUSE OTHERS

By the late 1980s, however, there was still little or no discussion in this country about the management and treatment needs of much younger sexual abusers, the problem not having been characterised or officially recognised. Nevertheless, the increased focus on child sexual abuse and on adult perpetrators of sexual abuse noted above probably created a climate of professional and public sensitivity within which other 'discoveries' about the phenomenon of child sexual abuse were more likely. As Corby (2000) argues, the 1990s have been characterised by a broadening of concerns beyond intra-familial abuse into concerns about the sexual and other maltreatment of children outside the family, in residential care, in situations of organised abuse and, as an echo of concerns in the late nineteenth century, in relation to child prostitution.

Thus by the early 1990s two significant developments had occurred in this country in relation to children and young people who sexually abuse:

- some 30 lines of guidance (paragraph 5.24) on how to deal with abuse carried out by children or young people had been included in the second edition of *Working Together* (DoH, 1991);
- the National Children's Home's *Report of the Committee of Enquiry into Children and Young People who Sexually abuse Other Children* (NCH, 1992) had been published.

Together these two documents comprised the first official and semi-official guidance on the subject of children and young people involved in (sexually) abusing other children. The influences which led to the publication of these two documents are interesting.

Analysis suggests that a number of influences were at the forefront in placing the problem of children and young people who sexually abuse on the public agenda, alongside other concerns about the abuse of children inside and outside the family. Firstly, North American publications were providing evidence of a growing body of research and practice on the subject of young sexual abusers. One publication, edited by Ryan and Lane (1991), on juvenile sexual offenders was proving to be particularly influential. This volume included chapters on the history of the development of work with young sexual abusers in North America since the late 1970s, theoretical perspectives on the causes and consequences of such abuse, and models for the management, assessment and treatment of juvenile sex offenders. In Chapter 3, Ryan (1991) identifies the pressures behind these North American developments.

In the late 1970's, numerous studies were reporting a dismal prognosis in treatment for adults who molested children ... many clinicians ... reached the same conclusion: "We have to get these guys sooner" (Abel et al 1985; Groth 1977) ... Simultaneously, workers in juvenile corrections and human sexuality programs began to see that many of the juveniles committed or referred on lesser complaints had actually committed serious sexual offenses. Looking to the adult field for direction, clinicians struggled to develop the first offense-specific programs for adolescent sex offenders (Knopp 1983). (Ryan, 1991: p. 18)

Although a well written and well-received publication, Ryan and Lane's book obviously suffered, from the point of view of the English experience, from being based within the legislative and organisational contexts of welfare provision in North America. Clearly, systems for dealing with young sexual abusers in England had to address the very different legislative and organisational arrangements in place in this country.

Secondly, criminal statistics and research studies in England and elsewhere, which are discussed shortly, were apparently providing evidence that a significant proportion of reported sexual offences were being committed by children and young people.

Thirdly, as Tom White, then NCH Chief Executive, commented in the introduction to the NCH Report (1992):

Staff in the National Children's Home have become increasingly aware of the problem, as have staff in other voluntary organisations and local authorities.(NCH, 1992: p. v)

Certainly subsequent research, which will be discussed later, indicates that the concerns of 'front-line' staff in both field and residential settings about young sexual abusers have played an important 'bottom-up' role in raising awareness of 'the problem' and increasing the pressure to develop policy, models of practice, and training and support for professionals working directly with such youngsters.

Finally, a small number of well placed organisations and certain key individuals within them also appear to have been influential in raising awareness about children and young people who sexually abuse and in influencing policy and practice initiatives. These include: NOTA, the National Organisation for the Treatment of Abusers; the Department of Health and one Social Services Inspector in particular; and various voluntary sector children's organisations. These influences are discussed in turn.

NOTA was, and remains, a key player in drawing attention to the problem of young sexual abusers and in contributing to training and the dissemination of information. NOTA, which has always been aimed at those directly involved in work with sexual offenders, began its life as ROTA (Regional Organisation for the Treatment of Abusers) in the north west of England in 1989. The organisation provides a self-help training and support network for front-line professionals across voluntary and statutory welfare agencies involved in work with sex offenders. Its membership includes those from child protection focused agencies, as well as professionals from youth justice and probation settings, psychologists and psychiatrists. In September 1991 ROTA expanded to become a national organisation, now having charitable status. Originally, the focus of the organisation's work was on the management and treatment of adult sex offenders. However, by the early 1990s, attention was also being paid to young sexual abusers, particularly male adolescents. In addition to publishing a Newsletter, NOTANews, and a refereed journal, *The Journal of Sexual Aggression*, NOTA was sponsoring workshops organised by local branches and a national annual conference, often involving keynote speakers from North America, such as Gail Ryan. All of these initiatives were helping to raise the profile of work with children and young people who sexually abuse.

Along with other professional groupings and welfare agencies, central government departments such as the Department of Health (DoH) and the Home Office were also increasingly focusing on the need to intervene with sex offenders, in order to prevent child sexual abuse. At some point between 1989 and 1991 one particular Social Services Inspector (SSI) in the Department of Health contacted the chair of ROTA, about another organisation, BASPCAN (British Association for the Study and Prevention of Child Abuse and Neglect), which was thinking of setting up a focus group or organisation on sex offenders (Morrison, 1997). The SSI did not know of ROTA and, as a result of her discussion with the chair, concluded that ROTA was already providing such a focus group, ahead of any initiative by BASPCAN. Consequently, when NOTA was established as a national organisation, the chair contacted the SSI about the possibility of government observers being involved. The SSI herself attended NOTA National Executive Committee meetings as an observer for some years, together with a representative from the Home Office.

Last, but not least, since the early 1990s some of the biggest children's charities - Barnardos, National Children's Home (NCH), NSPCC, ChildLine and Save the Children - have played a major role in relation to the problem of young sexual abusers. This has been in terms of both contributing to discussions and debate on the problem and making a major contribution to the development of some of the earliest projects. These have specialised in providing a service for such youngsters, often through time limited initiatives, funded through service level agreements with social services departments.

All the above factors, then, in a context of heightened awareness and concern about (adult) sex offending and a broadening of concerns about other aspects of child abuse which have been identified earlier, contributed, it can be argued, to the emergence of the identification of the problem of children and young people who sexually abuse in England since the early 1990s.

CHAPTER 2
RESEARCH AND LITERATURE ON CHILDREN AND YOUNG PEOPLE WHO SEXUALLY ABUSE

A NOTE ON DEFINITIONS AND TERMINOLOGY

Defining what is sexually abusive behaviour by children and young people emerges as problematic. A number of publications have struggled with the problem of trying to differentiate normal sexual exploration in childhood from inappropriate sexual behaviour and sexually abusive behaviour (Pithers et al, 1983; NCH, 1992; O'Callaghan and Print, 1994; Ryan and Lane, 1997; Brown, 1999). This is not an easy task and, as Ryan (1999) comments:

> *in defining the sexual abuse of children by adults, age and behaviour are sufficient identifiers (i.e., if an adult does something sexual to a child, it is defined as sexual abuse); however, the definition of abuse perpetrated by children and adolescents requires additional descriptors.* (Ryan, 1999: p. 424)

The National Children's Home Committee of Enquiry (NCH, 1992) discussed key factors, such as consent, power imbalance (as opposed to equality) and exploitation or coercion, that need to be borne in mind when deciding whether what has happened between two minors is sexually abusive and the definition offered by Ryan and Lane (1997) is often quoted at training events and in other literature:

> *Sexually abusive behaviour has been defined as any sexual interaction with person(s) of any age that is perpetrated (1) against the victim's will, (2) without consent, or (3) in an aggressive, exploitative, manipulative or threatening manner.* (Ryan and Lane, 1997: p. 3)

Checklists such as those offered by Ryan and Lane (1997), and O'Callaghan and Print (1994) or the list of questions generated by the NCH Enquiry Report (1992, paragraph 2.8) may also assist in the process of decision-making. It would appear, however, that professional judgements will always be involved in coming to conclusions about what is or is not abusive behaviour. The NCH Committee of Enquiry concluded that such judgements should be based on an investigation by social services and/or the police and an assessment of the circumstances of the incident under child protection procedures (NCH, 1992, paragraph 2.10). Similarly, Corby (1993) comments in his publication focusing on child abuse committed by adults that:

> *... the only safe definition of child abuse is that it is a conclusion reached by a group of professionals on the examination of the circumstances of a child, normally (in Britain) at a case conference. Such a definition is usually symbolised by the placing of the child's name on a child protection register.* (Corby, 1993: p. 42-43)

However, in relation to sexual aggression or sexual abuse committed by children or young people such a process of construction is problematic because, as the empirical research evidences, despite official guidance that such youngsters should be dealt with under child protection procedures, many alleged young abusers were not being considered within such procedures and even today current DoH registration categories do not anyway provide for children and young people to be registered as (sexual) abusers.

As regards terminology, there appears to be a range of phrases used to refer to children and young people who are sexually aggressive or abusive towards others, phrases which have fallen in and out of professional favour since the early 1990s.

The National Children's Home Enquiry Report (NCH, 1992) in paragraphs 1.5 and 1.6 acknowledged the dilemmas with regard to terminology and commented:

[The Committee] recognises the need for continued debate on this issue. Such a debate must take into account the different professional and national contexts in which work with young sex abusers takes place. (NCH, 1992: p. 2)

A telephone interview with one of the members of the Committee (8 June, 1999) indicated that this measured statement did not do justice to the heated debate which occurred on the subject at the opening session of the Committee deliberations. Her memory was that the Committee had anticipated that agreeing on terminology would be an easy matter but a 'fraught discussion' had ensued. Various terms, for example 'sexual abusers' 'sexually aggressive' or 'over sexualised' children, had been considered and rejected, either because members had been concerned about the dangers of placing adult-like labels on youngsters inappropriately, or because the phrases suggested did not accurately delineate the problem. Thus, for example, it was acknowledged that the term 'over sexualised' could apply to a victim as much as to a perpetrator. The phrase finally agreed on by the Committee, children and young people who sexually abuse other children, was apparently considered by some members as far too long and unwieldy but a necessary compromise. Even now this debate on terminology is apparently ongoing, as evidenced by the variety of terms used in published works (Hoghughi et al, 1997; Ryan and Lane, 1997; Erooga and Masson, 1999).

INCIDENCE AND PREVALENCE OF SEXUAL ABUSE BY CHILDREN AND YOUNG PEOPLE

Against the background outlined thus far any discussion of the incidence and prevalence of sexual abuse by children and young people is clearly problematic. In addition, as the following analysis of official and research statistics indicates, even such 'objective' figures cover a multitude of ambiguities. Nevertheless an attempt is made here to assess the current state of knowledge about the size of the problem of children and young people who sexually abuse others.

CRIMINAL STATISTICS

As an exemplar year, criminal statistics for England and Wales for 2000 (Home Office, 2001) give the recorded level of sexual offences as 37,311. This total comprises less than 1 per cent of all notifiable offences. It should also be noted that less than 1% of these 37,311 offences were committed by females. Out of the total of recorded sexual offences, 5,200 individuals were subsequently reprimanded or finally warned (if juvenile offenders) or cautioned (if adult) for a sexual offence or were found guilty of a sexual offence in a court of law. (Interestingly, 5,200 cautions and convictions in 2000 represent a steadily decreasing annual number from the 10,700 recorded in 1988 and 1989). Approximately 21 per cent (1,100) of the 5,200 were aged between 10 and 21 years of age. 1,300 of the 5,200 cautioned or found guilty were reprimanded, finally warned or cautioned. Of these, approximately 15 per cent (200) were aged 12 - 14 years, 15 per cent (200) were aged 15 - 17 years and 7.5 per cent (100) were aged 18 - 20 years. In other words, (predominantly male) children and young people aged between 10 and 21 years accounted for 38 per cent of all reprimands, final warnings and cautions for sexual offences. Of the approximately 3,900 males who were found guilty in a court of a sexual offence, 2.5 per cent (100) were aged 12 -14 years, 8 per cent (300) were aged 15 -17 years and 5 per cent (200) were aged between 18 and 20. Thus, a much smaller, but significant percentage of young people (15 per cent) accounted for findings of guilt as a result of court process, as compared with the percentage of young people accounting for reprimands and final warnings.

These official statistics, which refer only to young sexual abusers over the age of criminal responsibility and only to reported offences, are likely to represent just a small proportion of sexual abuse committed by children and young people, particularly as it is claimed (NCH,

1992) that much abuse goes unreported or is not recognised or dealt with as such. Moreover, as a number of commentators have powerfully argued (see, for example, Cicourel, 1967; Shipman, 1981; Scott, 1990; May, 1993), such ostensibly reliable data is, in fact, highly problematic given the tortuous and socially situated processes through which it is generated and the confusing and inconsistent nature of the data itself. Shipman (1981) comments:

> *To Cicourel, official statistics of juvenile crime are made up in the same way as rumour is generated and transmitted. Vague and discontinuous pieces of information are transformed into ordered occurrences.* (Shipman, 1981: p. 122)

PREVALENCE STUDIES

Various other kinds of studies have, therefore, attempted to estimate the extent of sexual abuse by young people. In a major retrospective study of adults concerning their experiences of abuse in childhood Finkelhor (1979) found that 34 per cent of women and 39 per cent of men who recalled having a sexual encounter during their childhood with someone five or more years older than themselves reported that the older partner was aged between 10 and 19 years. Other studies (Ageton, 1983; Fromuth et al, 1991) suggest that about 3 per cent of all adolescent males have committed sexually abusive acts, whilst Abel et al (1987) found that approximately 50 per cent of adult sex offenders they studied reported that they had had deviant sexual interests during their adolescent years.

Caution must always be applied when interpreting the results of such retrospective studies. For example, in the case of the Abel et al (1987) study, their findings can be misinterpreted as demonstrating high rates of adolescent sexual deviancy which get carried through into adulthood. It may instead be that many or indeed all adolescent males have deviant sexual interests but only a proportion act on those interests at the time or later in their lives. Research on this conjecture has yet to be conducted. Nevertheless, weighing up these kinds of statistical and research findings, overview reports (see, for example, Kelly et al, 1991; NCH, 1992; Openshaw et al, 1993; Grubin, 1998) consistently conclude that between about 25-33 per cent of all alleged sexual abuse involves young (mainly adolescent) perpetrators.

CURRENT FINDINGS ON THE CHARACTERISTICS OF CHILDREN AND YOUNG PEOPLE WHO SEXUALLY ABUSE

As the criminal statistics for 2000 (Home Office, 2001) seem to suggest, young sexual offenders are predominately males in their middle to late teenage years. Early literature (for example, NCH, 1992; Ryan and Lane, 1991) focused almost exclusively on male adolescents, having very little to say about other children. However, there are now significant concerns expressed in the literature about other groups of youngsters involved in sexually aggressive or abusive behaviour and an outline of their characteristics is provided below. Initially, however, the focus is on the largest category of young sexual abusers, adolescent males. It should be noted here also that current literature on the characteristics of young sexual abusers tends not to distinguish between those reported for intra-familial, as opposed to extra-familial abuse. Neither does literature appear to into account dimensions of race, ethnicity or sexual orientation when discussing the characteristics of young sexual abusers.

MALE ADOLESCENT SEXUAL ABUSERS

Based on existing published studies, it is argued in texts overviewing the terrain (see, for example, Barbaree et al, 1993, Morrison and Print, 1995; Ryan and Lane, 1997, Grubin, 1998) that a generalised picture of male adolescent sexual abusers and their offences can be developed.

The victims of such offenders are said to be usually younger by a number of years. They comprise both male and female children and are often, as is the case with adult child molesters, known to the abuser, for example as a sibling or through a baby-sitting relationship, although, in cases of rape, the abusers are apparently less likely to know their victims. Although the full range of sexually abusive behaviours identified in respect of adult sex offenders is also perpetrated by such youngsters, Ryan and Lane (1997) suggest:

> *The modal offence scenario most likely involves a seven or eight-year-old victim, and more likely a female who is not related to the offender by blood or marriage. The behaviour is unwanted, involves genital touching and often penetration (over 60 per cent), and is accompanied by sufficient coercion or force to overcome the victim's resistance.*
> (Ryan and Lane, 1997: p. 7)

In terms of their characteristics, and as literature on adult sex offenders also indicates, young male sexual abusers are typically portrayed as having a number of social skills deficits, often being described as socially isolated, lacking dating skills and sexual knowledge, and experiencing high levels of social anxiety. These conclusions are based on a rapidly increasing number of studies, both in North America and the UK, including a study of 305 offenders aged 18 years or younger by Fehrenbach et al. (1986), a study of 161 young sex offenders aged under 19 years by Wasserman and Kappel (1985), studies of 24 and 29 young child molesters aged under 16 years by Awad et al (1984) and Awad and Saunders (1989) respectively, a British study conducted by Manocha and Mezey (1998) of 51 adolescents, aged between 13 and 18 years and a database of over 1,600 adolescent sex offenders in North America which has been compiled by the National Adolescent Perpetrator Network (Ryan et al., 1996). Not surprisingly, this reported lack of social competence is seen as often resulting in low self-esteem and emotional loneliness. Some commentators point out, however, that low self-esteem may be a consequence of contemporary events, for example, being apprehended and punished although, for others, it may be a problem which is long-standing and chronic. Thus Marshall (1989) has suggested that problems of early emotional attachment contribute to a failure to establish intimate relationships in later life and subsequent low self-esteem and emotional loneliness.

Young male sexual abusers, it is asserted, may well be doing poorly at school both in terms of behaviour and educational attainment (see, for example, a study by Kahn and Chambers (1991) of 221 adolescent sex offenders) and, as in studies of adult male sexual offenders, relatively high proportions of them (between 25 per cent and 60 per cent, depending on the study cited) report having been victims of sexual abuse themselves (O'Callaghan and Print, 1994). A number of studies, therefore, also suggest that the families of such youngsters may have a number of difficulties in terms of their stability and intra-familial dynamics (Ryan and Lane, 1997).

Despite the fact that most research into young sexual abusers has focused on adolescent males there are many aspects of this population which warrant further study. Existing empirical studies are often flawed in that they do not adequately compare adolescent sexual abusers with either non-abusing adolescents or, for example, with violent and non-violent delinquents. In the case of those that do, the results are not clear cut, some studies suggesting that many of the characteristics just described are also common in the backgrounds of other violent and non-violent juvenile delinquents (see, for example, Bischof et al, 1995, Ryan, 1999) whereas other studies suggest some significant differences (see, for comparison, Ford and Linney, 1995; Katz, 1990). As Barbaree et al (1993) comment:

> *In all likelihood, the population of juvenile sex offenders is every bit as heterogeneous as the population of adult sex offenders.* (Barbaree et al, 1993: p. 16)

As in the case of adult sex offenders, some research has now begun to try and identify sub-groups within the total population, with a view to refining current assessment and treatment approaches. Thus, for example, Richardson et al (1997) have reported on their study in England of 100 male adolescent sex offenders aged 11 - 18 whom they categorised into 4 groups, on the basis of the age of their victims and the relationship between abuser and victim. They identified 4 groupings: a group of 31 child abusers (whose victims were 4 or more years younger than themselves); a group of 20 who abused their siblings; a group of 24 abusers who had assaulted same-aged or older victims and a mixed group of 22 subjects. Interestingly, the researchers found that 41% of the victims of the child group were male, about twice the rate of the mixed and incest groups. None of the peer group victims was male and, indeed, the backgrounds of the 'peer group' were found to be most similar to those of adult rapists. It would appear that further research in this area is needed and may prove fruitful in the future in distinguishing between different categories of male adolescent sexual abusers.

FEMALE ADOLESCENT SEXUAL ABUSERS

In their overview of female youth who sexually abuse, Lane with Lobanov-Rostovsky (1997) comment on the very disturbed backgrounds of the young female abusers with whom they have worked, noting high levels of both sexual and physical victimisation, problematic relationships with parents, family separation, problems at school and with peers in particular. However, they also comment:

Many of the developmental experiences are similar to those identified in the history of male youth, although they may be experienced differently by female youth based on gender, socialisation and role expectations. (Lane with Lobanov-Rostovsky, 1997: p. 348)

They and others (see, for example, Blues et al, 1999) suggest that young female sexual abusers may well benefit from the same kinds of treatment approaches as young male sexual abusers, although they comment that issues of autonomy and the consequences of female socialisation experiences may well be useful additional foci.

PRE-ADOLESCENT SEXUAL ABUSERS

As regards younger children, one of the earliest descriptions of sexually aggressive children in treatment (47 boys aged four-13 years) was provided by Johnson (1988). 49 per cent of these boys had themselves been sexually abused and 19 per cent were physically abused by people they knew. The boys all knew the children they abused. In 46 per cent of cases the victim was a sibling and 18 per cent were members of the extended family. Compared to adolescent sexual abusers it appeared that these sexually aggressive children used less coercion and more enticement to secure the compliance of their victims. The mean age of the boys at the time of their sexually aggressive behaviour was eight years nine months; the mean age of their victims was six years nine months. There was a history of sexual and physical abuse in the majority of the families of the boys, as well as a history of substance abuse.

In one of the few studies of female sexually aggressive children, also by Johnson (1989), it was reported that all of the sample of 13 girls (aged four to 12 years, with a mean age of 7.5) who were in treatment had been subjected to prior sexual victimisation of a serious nature, often with close relatives, and had usually received little support and validation from other family members when they had disclosed their abuse. 31 per cent had also been physically abused. All had used force or coercion to gain the compliance of their victims and 77 per cent had chosen victims in the family. The mean age of their first known sexually aggressive behaviour was six years, nine months and the average age of their victims was four years four months.

In a larger, more recent study of 287 sexually aggressive children aged 12 years and under (Burton et al, 1997) 79 per cent of the children were male and 21 per cent were female, with the average child living in a two parent home. In 70 per cent of their families at least one caretaker was chemically dependent; 48 per cent had at least one parent known to have been sexually abused; and 72 per cent of the children were sexually abused themselves (60 per cent by a carer). The children with known sexual abuse histories were younger at the first sign of sexual aggression than those without known sexual abuse histories.

Lane with Lobanov-Rostovsky (1997) have surveyed the issues and concerns raised by young children with sexually aggressive behaviour problems. They have worked with some 100 young children whom they divided into two treatment groups (seven-nine years and 10-12 years). The majority of these children were male and two thirds were white. Nearly half of the children were living at home at the point of referral and over two thirds had a history of sexual, physical or emotional victimisation or abandonment experiences. One third exhibited psychiatric, learning or medical problems and about a quarter had been involved in what would be considered other delinquent activity if they were older. Butler and Elliott (1999) also provide a helpful overview of treatment approaches to pre-adolescent sexually aggressive children.

YOUNG ABUSERS WITH LEARNING DIFFICULTIES

Lane with Lobanov-Rostovsky (1997) comment in relation to this group:

Clinical observation indicates numerous similarities but also some unique differences between sexually abusive behaviour of disabled and non-disabled youth. The range of behaviours, the types of sexually abusive behaviours, and the elements of the behaviour appear similar, while the associated cognitive processes, the context of the behaviours and the level of sophistication exhibit some differences. (Lane with Lobanov-Rostovsky, 1997: 342)

What little (empirical) research has been undertaken seems to suggest that there may be a more repetitive, habitual quality to the behaviour of these youngsters in terms of victim choice, location and frequency of behaviour. They may have greater difficulty understanding the abusive nature of their activities and may justify what they have done in terms of what they perceive to be normal male behaviour. They may also exhibit more impulsivity and a more childlike need for immediate gratification.

Stermac and Sheridan (1993) suggest that young abusers with learning difficulties are significantly more likely to display inappropriate, non-assaultive 'nuisance' behaviours such as public masturbation, exhibitionism and voyeurism and that they are less discriminating in their choice of victim, choosing male and female victims equally. It can be argued that their behaviour also has to be understood in the context of societal prejudice towards such disability, a general lack of attention paid to issues of sexuality in relation to this group and their increased vulnerability to being the victims of sexual abuse themselves. Thus, it is argued, management and treatment of these young people has to be planned in the light of careful assessment of their cognitive and social functioning so that, for example, treatment delivery attends to issues such as shortened attention spans, more experiential styles of learning and the need for careful use of language and repetition of messages.

CHAPTER 3
THEORIES OF CAUSATION AND THE FOCUS OF CURRENT TREATMENT APPROACHES

Various texts (NCH, 1992; Sampson, 1994; Hoghughi et al, 1997; Ryan and Lane 1997 and Corby, 2000) have overviewed the range of theories put forward to explain sexual abuse generally, including sexual abuse perpetrated by children and young people. Thus, for example, Ryan and Lane (1997) provide an historical account of how sexual aggression has been variously explained by reference to psychosis (or insanity), physiology (due to the influence of neurological and/or hormonal factors); intrapsychic conflict (based on Freudian ideas); learning theory (sexual aggression as learned behaviour, based on instrumental and observational learning); attachment theory (sexual aggression as symptomatic of failures or deficits in early and later attachment); cognitive theory (sexual aggression as resulting from distorted and/or irrational patterns of thinking); addictive theory (sexual aggression as compulsive behaviour requiring similar intervention as with alcohol addiction) and family systems ideas (that family interrelationships and dysfunction cause sexual abuse, particularly in respect of father-daughter incest). The NCH Enquiry Report (1992) Sampson (1994) and Corby (2000) also draw attention to broader sociological perspectives on the causes of sexual aggression, such as structural explanations rooted in a feminist analysis of patriarchal society.

However single theories about the causes of sexual aggression are probably less helpful than theories which attempt to integrate these ideas, combining elements from sociological, psychological and biological perspectives. Thus in 1984 Finkelhor was criticising existing theory on three main counts. Firstly, he argued that two very different types of theory had been emerging - about (often extra-familial) child molesters on the one hand and about the specific family dynamics of father-daughter incest on the other – with little attempt to collate what was known about offenders (based on the work of psychologists with incarcerated offenders) with emerging theory and research about intra-familial father-daughter incest, largely conducted by child protectionists. Secondly, none of the available theory was particularly helpful in explaining sexual abuse by, for example, older brothers, other relatives and family friends and acquaintances. Thirdly, Finkelhor argued, available theory, which was based on clinical practice, neglected sociological dimensions which were important in explaining what was a widespread social problem (Finkelhor, 1984). Thus he proposed a comprehensive model which aimed at addressing these shortcomings, without being specific to a particular school of thought about aetiology.

FINKELHOR'S FOUR-PRECONDITIONS MODEL

Finkelhor's model (set out in Figure 1.1) related primarily to adult male abusers but it is frequently adapted in practice for use with adolescents.

Figure 1.1   Finkelhor's 4 Pre-Conditions Model (Finkelhor, 1984)

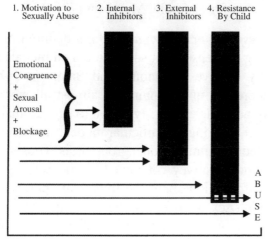

In summary, the model suggests four preconditions which must be met before sexual abuse can occur. The potential abuser needs to:

1) have some motivation to abuse – this may be because the victim meets some important emotional need and/or sexual contact with the victim is sexually gratifying and/or other sources of sexual gratification are not available or are less satisfying;

2) overcome any internal inhibitions against acting on that motivation – commonly this is by way of 'cognitive distortions', self-serving distortions of attitude and belief, whereby the victims, either individually or as a 'category' become seen as in some way consenting to or responsible for their own abuse;

3) overcome external inhibitors to committing sexual abuse – gaining the opportunity to have access to the potential victim in an environment where the abuse is possible. In the case of child victims this may relate to the supervision the child receives from others;

4) overcome or undermine a victim's possible resistance to the abuse: – writing in relation to child victims, Finkelhor argues that this is not an issue to be regarded simplistically but may relate to a complex set of factors involving personality traits which inhibit the targeting of a particular child as well as more straightforward resistance to the abuse itself. These concepts, he suggests, are equally applicable to peer or adult victims.

What is suggested, therefore, is that there are a number of potential barriers to abuse, the first two relating to the abuser and the third and fourth relating to factors external to the abuser. Thus the model claims to offer a way of beginning to understand something of the dynamics of the abuser as well as the abuse process.

When discussing factors associated with the development of sexually abusive behaviour in children and young people specifically, Becker (1988) proposed a similar model which included a broad range of factors which may contribute to the development of sexually abusive behaviour:

- at an individual level: social isolation; impulse conduct disorder; limited cognitive abilities and a history of physical and/or sexual abuse;

- familial factors: carers who engage in coercive sexual behaviour; family belief systems supportive of such behaviour and carers who have poor interpersonal skills and lack empathy; and

- societal factors: society which is supportive of coercive (male) sexual behaviour; society which supports the sexualisation of children and peer groups who behave in anti-social ways.

More recently Swenson et al (1998) have proposed the adoption of a multi-systemic model of treatment in relation to work with young sexual abusers, similarly based on an appreciation of the many variables which may contribute to the development of such behaviour. Such ideas are echoed in more recent literature, see, for example, Morrison (2001).

Current intervention approaches in respect of children and young people who sexually abuse
Whilst there appears to be an emerging consensus that such integrated models are important in understanding the causes of sexually abusive behaviour (and Sampson (1994) claims that Finkelhor's model comprises the theoretical underpinning of almost all work with adult sex offenders in the British penal system), nevertheless surveys seem to suggest that many treatment programmes are more narrowly focused, drawing on particular models, and tending to work with individuals, either on a one to one or more commonly on a group basis. Thus, for example, Ryan and Lane (1997) report on a 1994 national survey conducted by the Safer Society (Freeman-Longo et al, 1995) which gathered information about the treatment approaches of 1784 programmes for child, adolescent and adult sex offenders in the USA. 281 (41% of respondents) indicated they used a cognitive-behavioural model, 247 (36%) identified relapse prevention as

their model of choice, with the remaining 156 respondents identifying psycho-educational (14%), psychotherapeutic (5%), family systems (2%), sexual addictive (1%) and psychoanalytical (1%) approaches respectively. As will be evident, cognitive-behavioural and relapse prevention models appear to dominate and so further detail about these models, which typically co-exist within treatment programmes, is provided below.

Lane's sexual abuse cycle - and its application to work with young sexual abusers
Clinical experience of treatment work with adolescents (Lane and Zamora, 1982, 1984) has led to the development of the concept of sexual abuse cycles involving dysfunctional responses to problematic situations or interactions. In these models, which are derived from Wolf's model (1984) (used in work with adult sex offenders), it is argued that such responses are based on distorted perceptions relating to power and control which then become sexualised. This framework is now claimed to be generally applicable irrespective of age or level of intellectual or developmental functioning and is reported to be in use, with appropriate adaptations to meet individual circumstances or need, in the majority of treatment programmes (Lane, 1997a).

The widespread use of this model in work with young people clearly indicates the intuitive and practice based appeal of this concept for exploring and understanding patterns of sexually abusive behaviour. However, even within a purely clinical and empirical context, the question of the validity of the model has yet to be established. Lane (1997a), a psychiatric nurse by training, argues, nevertheless, that research has begun to confirm various elements of the cycle model, most recently the link between negative affective states and deviant sexual fantasy.

The sexual abuse cycle for adolescents set out in Figure 1.2 (Lane, 1997a) is said to represent cognitive and behavioural progressions prior to, during and after sexually abusive behaviour. When applied to an individual, the details of the components of the cycle may vary, but it is argued that elements of the overall pattern are still apparent, with common abusive behaviour patterns, types of gratification and styles of thinking which support the behaviour.

However, in using the model it is stressed by proponents that it should be seen as describing a process of events, not a causal representation. Typically, the model is represented cyclically because of the repetitive compulsive nature of the behaviour sequence and because of reported indications that previous abuse incidents often parallel and reinforce the subsequent abuse pattern.

Figure 1.2   The Sexual Abuse Cycle (Lane, 1997a: p. 80)

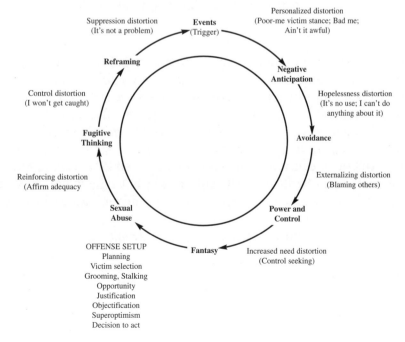

As shown diagrammatically in Figure 1.2, the young person's life experiences, outlook and beliefs are said to predispose them to respond to an event, interaction or problem with feelings of helplessness (the event), experienced as stressful and anticipated as unsafe (negative antici- pation). Feelings of hopelessness are then accompanied by a desire to avoid the issue, the feel- ings and the anticipated outcomes (avoidance). Not being successful in this leads, it is claimed, to feelings of resentment and defensiveness and attempts to exert power over oth- ers in a non-sexual way as compensation (power/control). Whilst effective, the duration of the effect is temporary, leading to thinking about further power-based behaviours and other behaviours which might feel good, such as sex (fantasy). The exertion of control or dominance is eventually expressed sexually (sexual abuse). There is, then, it is suggested, a need to cope with the knowledge of the behaviour and fear of external consequences of being caught (fugitive thinking). Inability to tolerate this anxiety or discomfort leads subsequently to the behaviour becoming assimilated through a series of cognitive distortions or 'thinking errors'. The cycle, therefore, is claimed to represent a series of maladaptive coping mechanisms that temporar- ily alleviate discomfort but do not resolve the problem.

The treatment implications of such models are held to be self-evident (Ryan and Lane, 1997). By becoming aware of his or her pattern of thinking, and emotional and behavioural responses through use of the cycle model, the young person can, then, it is argued, con- sciously develop other methods of coping with stress or abusive stimuli and thus decrease the likelihood of further abusive behaviour. Such focused, cognitive behavioural therapy is now seen as a key element of work with both adult and young sexual abusers in the UK (Beckett et al, 1994; Morrison et al, 1994; Will et al, 1994/1995; Hird and Morrison, 1996; Hoghughi et al, 1997; Erooga and Masson, 1999) covering such aspects as minimisation, denial and projection of blame; cognitive distortions; deviant sexual arousal; victim empathy and victim awareness; rape prone attitudes and beliefs and relapse prevention.

Whilst avoiding relapse is a goal of intervention from the outset, the young person's active participation in relapse prevention can, it is argued, increase as their understanding of their own process increases. Thus when an abuser understands his own cycle, it should then be possible for him to share this knowledge with relevant others, by developing his own alert checklist (North West Treatment Associates, 1988). From this he should be able to develop a relapse prevention plan with identified triggers, danger situations and strategies for coping with these prior to concluding any programme of intervention. Pithers and Gray (1996) have suggested that motivation to learn and use relapse prevention strategies increases once victim awareness is heightened and empathy work has been completed.

A CRITIQUE OF CURRENT MODELS OF INTERVENTION

It is important to appreciate that these current, preferred models and, indeed, the bulk of liter- ature about adult sex offenders and about children and young people who sexually abuse emanates from a strong tradition of clinical treatment and research undertaken particularly by psychologists, often originally based on work with adult sex offenders. Thus, for example, at the end of 1997 the 21 members of the editorial board of *Sexual Abuse: A Journal of Research and Treatment*, the official journal of the *Association for the Treatment of Sexual Abusers* (ATSA), the North American equivalent of NOTA, comprised 21 men and five women, seven of whom were medically qualified and 15 of whom had PhDs, the majority in psychology. 15 of the board members worked in clinical settings, 10 in universities and one was based in a government department.

Similarly significant book publications in the UK on the subject of adult sex offenders and on children and young people who sexually abuse also provide evidence of the dominance of clinical, particularly psychological, voices in current literature. Thus, four out of the nine con- tributors to the very well received UK publication *Sexual Offending Against Children: Assessment and Treatment of Male abusers* (Morrison et al, 1994) were clinical psychologists and all of the 10 contributors to *Working with Sexually Abusive Adolescents* (Hoghughi et al, 1997) were senior or consultant clinical or forensic psychologists with the exception of one who was a consultant forensic adolescent psychiatrist. Even a publication which was deliberately constructed to try and permit eminent voices from a range of subject disciplines and professional backgrounds to be heard (Erooga and Masson, 1999) was well represented by psychologists and psychiatrists who authored six out of the 13 chapters.

Literature on work with young sexual abusers, which, as has already been indicated, has developed from more established interests in, and experience of working with, adult sex offenders, therefore, tends to offer a perspective on the problem of children and young people who sexually abuse which is clinically driven and focused on individual pathology and treatment. Thus, wider social policy, sociological and other perspectives have been relatively invisible in the literature, including the perspectives of children themselves, as victims or as abusers.

For example, in relation to broader societal factors, and as has already been noted, existing studies indicate that sexual offending is largely perpetrated by males and any explanation of such offending could, therefore, be considered within a context of much larger, unreported rates of 'normal' male sexual aggression against females. Kelly et al (1992) argue that research on convicted offenders and theories of behaviour emerging from a clinical focus have tended to maintain the dominance of the medical/pathology perspective in relation to particular individuals. In doing so they fail to address social constructions of masculinity and prevalent societal attitudes and beliefs which condone or justify sexual violence against female adults and children which, if changed, would result in the transformation of family power relations.

THE 'CHILD' IN CHILDREN AND YOUNG PEOPLE WHO SEXUALLY ABUSE

A particular concern, which has recently been expressed about existing treatment models and interventions, is that they focus on children as 'abusers' to the exclusion of their other needs as children, adolescents, black or white people, males or females, heterosexual or gay individuals. Thus, it is argued, treatment can be applied in 'uncreative' ways, with anti-oppressive practice models in relation to this area of work very underdeveloped (Featherstone and Lancaster, 1997; Hackett, 2000).

However it may be that professional conceptualisations are changing in this respect. Thus, in one of her more recent articles, Ryan (1999) overviews what she describes as 'the evolving consensus' about the treatment of sexually abusive youth. Whilst recognising and supporting the influence of the models of treatment and interventions described above she also reports on:

> a growing recognition that the offense-specific interventions should recognise and address the realities of the developmental needs and deficits in a youthful population. In short, the view has altered to remember that the sexually abusive youth is still growing and to view the offending behaviour in the context of a more holistic developmental approach. (Ryan, 1999: p. 426)

Interestingly, the November 1998 issue of the journal *Child Maltreatment* was devoted to the topic of interventions with young sexual abusers and was introduced by an editorial entitled 'Don't Shoot, We're your Children: Have we gone too far in our responses to Adolescent Sexual Abusers and Children with Sexual Behavioural Problems?' (Chaffin and Bonner, 1998). The editorial goes on to question the wisdom or validity of basing responses to children and young people who sexually abuse on models developed to deal with adult offenders, often in penal settings.

THE ISSUE OF RECIDIVISM IN CHILDREN AND YOUNG PEOPLE WHO SEXUALLY ABUSE

Also on the basis of interpretation (and possibly misinterpretation as has already been mentioned) of the findings of studies of adult sex offenders (for example, Abel et al, 1987), early thinking, as reported in the NCH Enquiry Report (1992), was that, unlike other juvenile delinquents who typically grow out of their offending, young sexual abusers were more likely to continue in their abusive behaviour unless treated, preferably under some kind of civil or criminal legal mandate.

From a research perspective, however, findings since the mid 1990s have cast some doubt on such early thinking. For example, Will (1994) reported on an American conference where Jim Brieling from the National Institute of Mental Health was reviewing the available literature on the outcome of treatment programmes. Will commented in his write-up:

> Although there are only a handful of good studies in this area, most show that the re-offending rate is low at less than 10%. Now, while this could mean that treatment programmes are incredibly powerful, it is more likely that it means that the vast majority of offenders taken on for treatment are not going to re-offend again regardless of whether they have treatment or not. (Will, 1994: p. 52)

Becker (1998) also comments that the few robust recidivism studies that have been undertaken also indicate that the recidivism rates are low. Weinrott (1996) has conducted what is probably the most thorough review of adolescent sexual offender recidivism studies to date. He examined 22 treatment studies, although the majority followed up subjects for under five years and none used untreated control groups. Bearing these limitations in mind, Weinrott nevertheless concluded that it appeared that relatively few adolescents were charged with subsequent sexual crimes, two thirds of the studies reporting re-offence rates of under 10 per cent. In addition he concluded that it appeared that adolescent sexual offenders were also less likely than other delinquents to re-offend non-sexually. Clearly, however, more research is needed in this area, with a view to trying to identify those young sexual abusers who are at high risk of recidivism, as other studies now attempt to do in relation to adult sex offenders (Grubin, 1998).

In a UK based study Glasgow et al (1994) looked at all children alleged to have sexually abused children in the city of Liverpool during a twelve-month period. Interestingly, they found that:

> adolescents were more than twice as likely to be suspected of having sexually abused another child than any other comparable age band in *adulthood or childhood* (my italics) (Glasgow et al, 1994: p. 196)

As a consequence, they argue strongly for a more explicit developmental perspective on sexual offending across the life span, a perspective which seeks to understand different patterns of sexual behaviour at different points in the life cycle and the constellations of factors that might increase the risk of certain individuals exhibiting sexually abusive behaviour at a given period in their lives. They hypothesise, for example, that in adolescence, as opposed to young adulthood:

> abuse is more likely to occur in susceptible individuals because of a combination of the intense sexual drive which characterises the period, together with numerous opportunities to abuse offered by continuing membership of the world of childhood ...
> (Glasgow et al, 1994: 207)

This analysis, which does not appear to have been developed since either by the authors or by others (Glasgow, 1999), may now undergo a revival, given Ryan's more recent discussion (1999) on the need for child centred, developmental perspective.

CHAPTER 4
EMPIRICAL RESEARCH INTO POLICY AND PRACTICE DEVELOPMENTS IN RELATION TO YOUNG SEXUAL ABUSERS IN ENGLAND

Between 1994 and 2000 the author of this monograph conducted research into the development in England of policy, procedures and services for young sexual abusers, an area relatively neglected in much literature. Some of the findings from this research are already in the public domain (Masson, 1995a; 1995b; 1997; 1997/1998).This section outlines the aims of the research and summarises and analyses the findings.

RESEARCH AIMS

The research aims were as follows:
1. to collate and analyse official and semi-official guidance existing in England since the early 1990s on how welfare agencies should respond to the problem of children and young people who sexually abuse and to explore and understand the process of its emergence;
2. to explore and analyse the development of policy, procedure and services in local Area Child Protection Committee (ACPC) areas in England during the 1990s via:
    *   a 100% sample survey of ACPC annual reports for the period 1992-4;
    *   exploration and analysis of ACPC inter-agency guidance;
    *   semi-structured interviews with professionals in a small number of ACPC areas;
    *   a national survey by questionnaire of professionals involved in this area of work.

ANALYSIS OF OFFICIAL AND SEMI-OFFICIAL GUIDANCE

The initial phase of the research, collating and analysing official and semi-official guidance available in the early 1990s on how welfare agencies should respond to children and young people who sexually abuse, involved the analysis of two texts: the 30 lines of paragraph 5.24 of Working Together (DoH, 1991) which are reproduced in Appendix 1 and the much more substantive enquiry report published by the NCH (1992).

In both documents it was found that young sexual abusers were being conceptualised as different from other juvenile offenders in that they were perceived as tending to grow into their behaviour, rather than out of it. Thus there were fears that, unless managed and treated, they would become the adult sex offenders of the future. Clear statements were being made that all such young people should be dealt with under existing child protection procedures and that a legal mandate might well be required to ensure co-operation with treatment. Area Child Protection Committees (ACPCs) were also being identified as bodies which should be leading and co-ordinating the development of appropriate systems of response to children and young people who sexually abuse.

Critical analysis of these sets of guidance highlighted their respective assumptions and limitations, an important aspect being the complete neglect in paragraph 5.24 and the relative neglect within the NCH enquiry report of the existence of alternative youth justice systems for the processing of children and young people over the age of 10 years who were alleged to have committed sexual offences. It was also noted that subsequent attempts by a central government inter-departmental working party to develop more extensive guidance to address this complication appeared to have fallen victim to increasingly hostile and punitive statements emanating from the Home Office from the mid 1990s onwards about serious offenders generally and about sex offenders in particular.

As a result of studying these texts many questions about whether, and how, professionals and agencies might be addressing the messages and recommendations contained in the guidance were unanswered. For example, was there a shared consensus developing about there being a problem of children and young people who sexually abuse and its parameters? Were local areas aware of the official and semi-official guidance in existence? Was the child protection discourse outlined above uncontested? Was there agreement that all such youngsters should be dealt with within existing child protection procedures? How were issues of child protection registration being negotiated? What about youth justice procedures in respect of children over the age of criminal responsibility? Were models of policy and procedure emerging? Were assessment and treatment facilities being established? What issues in relation to young sexual abusers were uppermost for professionals, agencies and ACPCs? The second phase of the research, therefore, aimed at exploring and analysing the development of policy, procedures and services in local ACPC areas in England in relation to children and young people who sexually abuse.

STUDY OF ACPC ANNUAL REPORTS 1992-4 AND SUBSEQUENT YEARS

NB: The reader should note that the analysis of ACPC annual reports preceded major changes to local authority boundaries as a result of the establishment of new unitary authorities. By the late 1990s the number of local authorities in England had increased to approximately 150.

Based on a 100% sample of 106 ACPC annual reports for each of the reporting years 1992-3 and 1993-4, and set in the context of official summaries of reports for earlier and subsequent years (Pont, undated; Armstrong, 1995, 1996 and 1997) it was possible to show that during 1992-1993 there was a noticeable rise in the amount of attention being paid to the problem of children and young people who sexually abuse, although there was evidence from the 1993-4 reports that this rise was then levelling off. This increased attention, it was hypothesised, was due to the publication and dissemination of *Working Together* (DoH, 1991) and the NCH Enquiry Report (1992).

The research also demonstrated some interesting regional variations in levels of activity in respect of the problem of young sexual abusers. Specifically, DoH Northern Region ACPC areas had been more active in terms of developing responses to young sexual abusers early on in the decade, for reasons which seemed to connect with the geographical origins of ROTA/NOTA, the *National Organisation for the Treatment of Abusers*. However, by the middle of the decade it appeared that Central and Southern Region ACPCs had, largely, caught up in levels of activity. Thus, of the 17 'particularly active' areas identified, Central, Southern and Northern Regions appeared to have similar proportions of such ACPC areas within their boundaries (29%, 19% and 22% respectively). In comparison with the other three DoH regions, London Boroughs Region ACPCs evidenced low levels of activity in relation to the problem of children and young people who sexually abuse. Moreover, across all regions, there was apparent evidence which indicated that very little or nothing was happening about the children and young people who sexually abuse in a substantial minority of English ACPC areas.

The 1993-4 ACPC annual reports indicated that approximately 30% of all ACPC areas were reporting that they had policies and procedures in place to manage children and young people referred because of their sexually abusive behaviour, with 59% claiming that they were in the process of developing them. As far as could be gleaned from these reports it appeared that such policies and procedures were being developed within the context of paragraph 5.24 of *Working Together* (DoH, 1991), with very few references in the ACPC annual reports to the relevance of youth justice systems of response in respect of children aged over 10 years.

A small number of the ACPC reports studied referred to issues that were exercising professionals in their areas: how to define what constituted sexual abuse by children and young people; whether it was valid to assume that young sexual abusers were likely to grow into rather than out of their behaviour; concerns about the number of referrals of very young children for alleged sexual abuse; worries about, on the one hand, issues of denial and minimisation and, on the other hand, of labelling children as Schedule 1 offenders; concerns about peer abuse in residential accommodation and complaints about having insufficient resources to develop appropriate services.

ANALYSING ACPC INTER-AGENCY GUIDANCE

It was possible to access just over half (57 or 54%) of a possible 106 ACPC inter-agency guidance documents, with variable representation across the four DoH regions. The amount of text devoted to the subject of children and young people who sexually abused varied considerably, from 1/2 a page or less in 9% of the 57 documents studied to more than two pages in 54% of the documents, as did their contents.

Thus, it was not always clear whether the inter-agency guidance studied had been drawn up to address just child sexual abuse or child-on-child abuse more generally. Similarly, there was great variation over what (if any) definition of juvenile sexual abuse or other related guidance was provided. The claim that young sexual abusers were different from other young offenders and that policies of minimal intervention might be less appropriate in their case also appeared to be contested, judged by the evidence from the texts, and ACPC areas were taking varying positions on whether young sexual abusers should be registered under their existing child protection arrangements. In a minority of the ACPC sets of guidance there were also clear statements that 'looked after' children should receive the same service as children not in local authority care, with the possible implication that they had not done so previously.

In terms of the similarities in the sets of guidance, what emerged from the reading of ACPC inter-agency guidance was a central focus on trying to identify those children and young people at (high) risk of re-abusing in order to target resources on them. There was evidence of a somewhat uncritical acceptance of the effectiveness of available risk assessment models, reflecting a more widespread application of the language of risk, dangerousness and risk assessments in other areas of social welfare provision. Finally, the sets of guidance were similar in containing evidence of considerable debate around issues associated with the development of policies and procedures in relation to children and young people who sexually abuse, issues which had also surfaced during the study of ACPC annual reports and which were briefly referred to above.

In the analysis of ACPC inter-agency guidance it was found that different models of policy and procedure were emerging and a four model categorisation was used in order to summarise key aspects of this variability. 18 (31%) sets of inter-agency guidance had policies and procedures which were outlined purely within the context of child protection systems of response. 26 (46%) sets of guidance had developed policies and procedures which attempted to synchronise child protection and youth justice systems of response, with child protection procedures usually taking precedence over youth justice process. Nine sets of guidance (16%) had elected to develop policies and procedures which made explicit distinctions between the processing of children under and over the age of criminal responsibility, and an even smaller number (four or 7%) were pursuing policies and procedures which provided an alternative route to child protection processes, via meetings held under Section 17 of the Children Act 1989 (children in need). Thus, what became clear from the inter-agency guidance, which was not obvious from the ACPC annual reports, was that the majority of these ACPC areas were actively trying to dovetail child protection and youth justice systems of response in respect of children aged 10 years and over.

The strengths and limitations of these various models were assessed and the results of the analysis of these texts were compared with the results of the study of ACPC annual reports, especially in relation to the 17 particularly active areas which had been identified. It became apparent that such particularly active areas often supported a project specialising in work with young sexual abusers, although the future funding and staffing of such projects did not always seem secure.

SEMI- STRUCTURED INTERVIEWS IN SIX NORTHERN REGION ACPC AREAS

During 1994-5 semi-structured interviews were held with nine child protection or youth justice professionals in six ACPC areas, most of them in senior management positions in their respective agencies. The aims of these interviews were to develop a more detailed picture of developments in a small number of areas, to complement the documentary research undertaken in respect of all ACPC areas in England.

There were striking variations in developments across the six ACPC areas, variations which seemed to be associated with historical, organisational and personal/ professional differences at the local level. However, what also emerged were a number of common themes, many of which echoed the findings from the study of documents. These included continuing debates about how to define sexual abuse by children and young people, the problems of raising awareness amongst agencies, including the police, courts and the Crown Prosecution Service, about the particular needs of young sexual abusers and issues of staff training. Tensions between child protection and traditional youth justice approaches towards young offenders were in evidence, as well as the practical problems of dovetailing child protection and youth justice systems of response at the point of referral and subsequently.

Most of the interviewees had concerns about inadequacies in their local inter-agency guidance on policy and procedures in relation to children and young people who sexually abuse and, hence, about inconsistent approaches to their management. The circumstances in which child protection case conferences should be held on young sexual abusers and issues of child protection registration were a major issue for at least some of my interviewees, as well as concerns about a lack of specialist staff and residential resources to support (risk) assessment work and treatment programmes. The need to monitor the extent of sexually abusive behaviour by children and young people, how such cases were managed and the outcomes of intervention was seen as of importance, in contexts where there were underlying concerns about opening up an area of work which might result in demands for increased resources which were unlikely to be forthcoming.

NATIONAL SURVEY OF PROFESSIONALS BY QUESTIONNAIRE

102 professionals across England, from a number of disciplines and identified as having particular knowledge of, or involvement in, work with young sexual abusers, responded to a questionnaire sent to them in late 1995 which was designed to gather a range of information. Data were collected on the respondents themselves, the extent and nature of their involvement in work involving sexual abuse by children and young people and the extent to which post-qualifying training opportunities on the subject had been available to them. Their responses to two lists of vignettes of potential incidents of sexual abuse by a child

were elicited in order to explore their opinions on the incidents' seriousness or otherwise. Information about, and respondent views on, policy and procedure in relation to children and young people who sexually abuse in their local area were then collected and respondent views were sought on child protection and youth justice perspectives in relation to this field of work. Finally, there was space for respondents to identify issues that were of concern and/or priority for them in relation to work with young sexual abusers.

Most respondents, who were almost all white and often in senior practitioner or management positions, reported only modest amounts of involvement in work with children and young people who sexually abuse, although it appeared that, for some, the proportion of their workload focusing on this service user group was increasing. Although generally well qualified individuals, they also reported having had only very limited amounts of post-qualifying training in this area of work.

When asked to rank brief vignettes of possible incidents of sexual abuse by children and young people in terms of their relative seriousness, respondents provided evidence that they were often using similar criteria when deciding about the abusiveness or otherwise of a given set of circumstances, criteria which were also alluded to in professional literature. These included the age of the alleged abuser, the age differential between the alleged victim and abuser, whether the activity seemed consensual as opposed to coerced, and the nature of the alleged abuser's behaviour and whether violence was involved. However, it was also clear that there were wide differences of opinion between respondents about the relative seriousness of any given incident.

As with the semi-structured interviews, when asked about local policy and procedures, respondents provided ample evidence of considerable variation in the models of policy and procedures in respect of young sexual abusers which were developing in their respective areas. Moreover, 58% of the respondents expressed themselves dissatisfied or very dissatisfied with their local area arrangements for dealing with children and young people who sexually abuse, again identifying very similar concerns and issues to those which emerged from the documentary research and semi-structured interviews.

Very few respondents attended both child protection and youth juvenile liaison meetings in respect of young sexual abusers, typically attending one or the other kind of meeting. In contrast, a substantial minority of the young sexual abusers were being processed through, and therefore having to cope with, both systems. Considerable differences of view were highlighted when respondents were asked about child protection versus youth justice perspectives on how young sexual abusers should be managed, with some of this difference of view perhaps accounted for by professional background.

OVERARCHING THEMES

Thus, overall, the research indicated that, during the 1990s in England, there was a growing, although by no means unanimous, perception that there was a problem of children and young people who sexually abuse, about which something needed to be done. However, the official or semi-official child protection discourse on the nature of the problem and how it should be handled as evidenced in paragraph 5.24 of Working Together (DoH, 1991) or the NCH Enquiry Report (NCH, 1992) was not universally shared. Indeed, what emerged from the field research, and from the earlier study of documentary data sources, was that this area of work was characterised both by a lack of resources and by significant issues and uncertainties which are outlined below.

As regards resources, there were concerns about a lack of initial and comprehensive assessment facilities, about too few treatment services and about poorly trained and unsupported staff. Particular worries were raised about the lack of placement options which often resulted in victims and abusers living in the same residential accommodation, with the vulnerability to abuse of 'looked after' children often highlighted. Doubts were also being expressed about the appropriateness of existing assessment and treatment facilities in the context of little monitoring, evaluation and research.

Public expenditure cuts were having impacts on a whole spectrum of welfare services during the 1990s and, therefore, concerns about resource issues can perhaps be explained relatively easily as one aspect of a more general problem. However, it could be conjectured that, in some areas, a lack of progress in accessing appropriate resources might be indicative of denial and minimisation of the problem on the part of those holding the purse strings. Certainly, this was implied by a few of the respondents although others commented that failure to secure resources merely reflected more general concerns about opening up new areas of work in a climate of resource constraint.

However, in addition to the resource problems, the data sources also highlighted professional concerns about more fundamental and conceptual issues which connected to ongoing problems associated with the implementation of policy and procedures and the development of services. Thus, issues which were regularly raised included the extent to which the problem really existed; whether it was possible to agree what was sexually abusive behaviour as compared to sexual experimentation or sexually inappropriate behaviour; whether this was behaviour that youngsters would grow out of or into; whether and how responses should be tailored to the age of the child; and how young abusers should be reacted to: as victims/abusers or both. The more pragmatic but associated issues that were regularly identified centred on the difficulties of dovetailing child protection and youth justice systems and the problems raised when processing 'abusers' through child protection systems created for children as victims.

The majority of these issues and concerns were addressed by the NCH Enquiry Report (1992) yet it appeared that, some years later, they were still high on professional agendas with limited evidence of a shared perception emerging. It was concluded, therefore, that, in order to understand the contested nature of the issues that were being voiced and the problems of dealing with young sexual abusers within existing child protection and youth justice systems, excursions were needed into broader conceptual frameworks.

CHAPTER 5
UNDERSTANDING THE PROBLEM OF YOUNG SEXUAL ABUSERS WITHIN BROADER CONCEPTUAL FRAMEWORKS

NOTIONS OF CHILDHOOD

It has been argued (Aries, 1962) that social constructions of childhood first emerged in the eighteenth century and there has been considerable debate since about the significance of this development. The construction of a category of childhood can be viewed as symbolic of a more caring society wishing to make specialised and humane provision for young people but others argue (for example Hendrick 1994 and 1997 and McGillivray, 1997) that this phenomenon can also be seen as the beginnings of more pervasive (modern) forms of social control or regulation of children and (particularly poor) families. Such general conceptualisations are very important for understanding the particular case of young sexual abusers and associated policy and practice developments, as will be discussed shortly. The focus for the moment will be on dominant adult conceptualisations of the nature of children.

DEPRIVED OR DEPRAVED?

More recent sociological studies of childhood (see, for example, James and Prout, 1997) emphasise that childhood as a social construction must be analysed in relation to variables of class, gender, ethnicity and power and that, in this process, children's own perceptions of their lives and social relationships must be heard. However, up until the emergence of these modern sociological analyses of childhood, conceptualising childhood has been very much the domain of adults who have largely ignored such variables in their analyses. These adult conceptions of the nature or principal identities of children have fluctuated in detail over time in response to significant events, political imperatives and the interests of dominant (primarily white, middle class, western) groups such as religious leaders, educationalists, medics, psychologists and others. However Jenks (1996) argues that, throughout history and across cultures, there appear to have been two over-arching or dominant ways of conceptualising or imagining the child: what he calls the Dionysian conception (the child as initially evil, corrupt and in need of surveillance and curbing) and the Appollonian conception (the child as innocent, untainted, needing nurturance, caring and protection). He comments:

> ... these images are immensely powerful, they live on and give force to the different discourses that we have about children; they constitute summaries of the way we have, over time, come to treat and process children 'normally'.(Jenks, 1996: p. 74)

Jenks argues that the Appollonian child has been the dominant conception in modern society, perhaps enshrined currently in the Children Act 1989 and he explains the emergence of child abuse as a 'new' problem since the 1970s and 1980s within this context. Thus, although there is well documented evidence of chronic exploitation of and violence against children throughout history, he argues that current preoccupations with the problem of child abuse are associated with increased levels of concern and caring for children and lower tolerance for their mistreatment. He claims, in some synchrony with the account provided earlier, that the heightening of concern for children as innocent victims of abuse was originally driven by two primary agencies: the women's movement's discourse on male violence and the child protection movement's construction of dysfunctional families and cycles of abuse. Continuing Appollonian conceptions, together with even more recent post modern nostalgic perceptions of children as unequivocal sources of love and trust, as constants in a world full of uncertainty and transitory relationships and as our investment in the future, have resulted in increasingly negative reactions to child abuse and maltreatment. As Jenks comments:

> *To abuse the child today is to strike at the remaining, embodied vestige of the social bond and the consequent collective reaction is, understandably, both resounding and vituperative.*(Jenks, 1996: p. 109)

If Jenk's argument that Appollonian social constructions of children have been dominant through much of the late twentieth century is accepted, then the 'discovery' of sexual abuse by children and young people in the early 1990s can be seen as problematic in a context where children are predominantly seen as innocent, angelic and untainted. Outrage and punitive responses against adult perpetrators of child abuse are common but how does one react to children accused of the same kinds of behaviour? In such circumstances, it is suggested, denial and minimisation of what has happened, or punitive, rejecting responses can easily be extremes along a continuum of anxiety driven adult coping strategies. The empirical research described earlier indicated that issues of denial and minimisation were perceived both as commonplace and of concern by many of the respondents. As regards the other end of the continuum, perhaps the demonising of Jon Venables and Robert Thompson, the young killers of Jamie Bulger, as monsters and evil freaks by the media and members of the public alike (Franklin and Horwath, 1996; Jenks, 1996; McGillivray 1997; Muncie, 1999a) provides a good illustration of the punitive, rejecting responses of commentators who could only conceive of these two children as something other than human.

This is despite an increasing body of evidence which suggests that exploitative and violent behaviour against children is regularly perpetrated by their peers, both by family members and by strangers (see, for example, O'Brien, 1989; Ambert, 1995; Fineran and Bennet, 1998, Gelles, 1997; Varma, 1997; Wiehe, 1997) and that, perhaps, more measured responses might be appropriate. However, whilst it has long been acknowledged that children are capable of harming each other, at least emotionally and physically, this behaviour has usually been labelled as something other than child abuse, for example, bullying (Olweus, 1978 and 1993; La Fontaine, 1991; Department for Education, 1994) and a part of normal childhood development. Parents are typically urged to curb the excesses of such behaviour as part of their efforts to discipline their offspring and to bring them up to maturity, and others involved in the care of children, such as teachers, are also expected to be vigilant about dealing with such ordinary problems.

In the last few years literature has begun to appear which attempts to reconstruct some of this child-on-child behaviour as abusive and, hence, implicitly or explicitly, as a child protection matter. Thus Ambert (1995) proposes a theory of peer abuse (verbal, physical and sexual), arguing that such abuse has to be explained and responded to in terms of individual/psychological factors and in terms of social and cultural environments which condone and reward it. Similarly, Dutt and Phillips (1996) present a powerful case for redefining racial harassment in general (but including attacks by children on their peers) as child abuse and, hence, something requiring a child protection response. Blyth and Cooper (1999) have also argued that bullying in schools might be addressed as a child protection issue and the Department for Education and Employment (1995) has already suggested that in extreme circumstances bullying could represent significant harm as defined by the Children Act,

1989, hence, requiring a response within child protection procedures. Most recently the NSPCC funded prevalence study (Cawson et al, 2000) provides powerful evidence of the extent of peer abuse, including sexual abuse, with the authors commenting:

> *These findings raise a number of questions about the ways in which we socialise young people in groups, manage their contacts with each other and educate them into expected behaviour with peers.*(Cawson et al, 2000: p. 95)

Ryan's attempt (1999) to broaden discussion of sexually abusive youth to cover the whole range of what she describes as 'abusive disorders', is of a similar construction. It can be argued, perhaps, that what is emerging here is a new discourse on child abuse which takes into account abuse by people under the age of majority. Whether these kinds of re-conceptualisations take hold in public and professional imaginations and what their impacts might be on how children and young people are responded to, remain to be seen, researched and analysed.

CHILDHOOD SEXUALITY

Similarly, understanding the nature of theorising about human sexuality and, in particular, acknowledging the dearth of knowledge and theorising in respect of childhood sexuality, is helpful when discussing the problem of children and young people who sexually abuse in general and the slow development of policy, procedure and services for such youngsters in particular.

Corby (1998) overviews the extensive knowledge base about adult sexuality which professionals could draw on in order to inform their work in child sexual abuse cases. This ranges from Freud's theory of psycho-sexual development (1978), through studies of adult sexual behaviour by, for example, Kinsey et al (1948 and 1953) and Masters and Johnson (1966 and 1970) and on to more social constructionist analyses of sexuality, such as that provided by Foucault (1979) and post modernist analyses of multiple sexualities (see, for example, Meyer, 1996).

However, so far as children are concerned, there is a dearth of literature and, what there is, is often couched in negative terms. Even in the case of adults, sexuality is an emotionally charged topic area at the best of times and childhood sexuality in particular:

> *is seldom treated as a strong or healthy force in the positive development of a child's personality...*(Martinson,1997: p. 36)

On the contrary, childhood sexuality is often dealt with very inadequately in textbooks (Yates 1982) and is often associated with pathology so that, for example, masturbation is seen as problematic behaviour. The proper adult role is often seen as protecting children from sexual matters, with assumptions made about the asexuality of pre-adolescents at least. Consequently there is a dearth of research which asks children themselves about their sexual knowledge, behaviour and emotions, research which involves children as subjects of their experience, Goldman and Goldman's publication (1988) being one of the few exceptions. Meyer (1996) also makes the point that the sexuality of less powerful groups such as women and children are typically defined within a dominant white, male, heterosexual social discourse and she provides a powerful social constructionist analysis of the limitations of the research and theoretical ideas of Freud and Kinsey as exemplars of such a discourse. It is not even universally agreed what the goals of sexual development are, what sexual maturity comprises. One of the few definitions of healthy sexual development which avoids gendered assumptions about the importance of male genital orgasm is offered by Barbaree et al (1993) and reads:

(Sexual maturity is)...the individual's integration of sexuality into an interpersonal context so that the sexual and personal needs, goals and rights of both self and other are compatible (Barbaree et al, 1993: p. 88)

What seems clear, however, from the research that *has* been undertaken (see, for example, Wade and Cirese 1991, Barbaree et al, 1993 and Martinson, 1997) is that children are sexual beings and that sexual development takes place throughout the life cycle. Various lines of development are involved including physiological/biological; emotional; cognitive; gender identity; socialisation and interpersonal development. Some writers (Hanks, 1994) suggest that early sexual behaviour is for comfort, pleasure and exploration and that cognitive developments are needed before these behaviours become imbued with adult-like meanings and significance. Certainly complex processes are involved in the development of sexual maturity. These include becoming sexually active and yet also responding to strong moral prohibitions; enjoying sensual intimacy which is, for example, acceptable between infants and mothers but understanding that such intimacy is not so straightforwardly acceptable otherwise; and negotiating 'do as I say not as I do' prescriptions from adults.

The research already cited (see, for example, Goldman and Goldman, 1988; Meyer, 1996; Wade and Cirese, 1991) also indicates that there are a tremendous range of normal sexual behaviours in children and that children's knowledge, behaviour and affect are affected by variables of age, class and gender as well as by societal and cultural differences. Smith and Grocke in their study (1995) found considerable variation in sexual knowledge across children's age groups and a wide range of behaviours, with consistent and pervasive differences according to social class and, to a lesser extent, gender. Moreover behaviours thought to be indicative of sexual abusive situations such as excessive masturbation, over-sexualised behaviour, an extensive curiosity or sexual knowledge and genital touching, were found to be common in the 'normal' community group of families they had studied as a contrast with families where sexual abuse had occurred.

However what also emerges from research is that whilst children and adolescents are very interested in sexual matters, they usually have to develop sexual knowledge and understanding for themselves, on their own and with their peers, because of the discomfort and prohibitions of adults. For example Plummer (1990) describes various processes which compound the difficulty for children in making sense of their sexuality. These include:

- scripting of absences – where adults don't help children with a vocabulary through which to discuss their struggles;
- scripting of values – children quickly learn that sexuality is value laden, and often negatively laden;
- scripting of secrecy – that sexual matters should not be public;
- scripting of the social uses of sexuality – children learn from adult behaviour that sexuality can be used in a variety of ways – for play, to express anger, to challenge authority, to exploit others and for pleasure.

The embarrassment and discomfort of adults is not confined to parents. Evidence suggests that there is a lack of professional training about childhood sexuality and about working with children on sexual issues (NCH, 1992; Farmer and Pollock, 1998) and so many workers and their supervisors feel very ill-prepared for direct, detailed work with children around these issues, particularly if they carry unresolved uncertainties and negativities from their own childhoods.

Given the above, one can appreciate how professionals may struggle, for example, to come to shared agreements about the differences between sexual experimentation, sexually inappropriate and sexually abusive behaviour in situations where sexual abuse by children and young people is alleged. Similarly it is also probably not surprising if some children and young people grow up with both low levels of sexual knowledge and/or with attitudes and perceptions which may be of concern to many carers and welfare professionals.

Green (1998), for example, in her ethnographic study of two residential children's homes discusses the often inaccurate and distorted sexual knowledge which the children and young people displayed, which they had learned from their peers, the media and sometimes from their own sexual victimisation. She argues that their sexual attitudes and behaviour appeared inextricably linked to their views on gender and how they thought men and women should naturally behave. Specifically, she perceived the young males in these homes as tending to objectify and sexually harass women and to talk about sexual matters in very physical, conquestual ways.

Obviously, the above illustration refers to youngsters in local authority accommodation who had been removed from their families for a variety of reasons and who evidenced various emotional and behavioural problems. One cannot argue, therefore, that their levels of sexual knowledge and their attitudes and behaviour are representative of those of all children and young people. However, the kinds of knowledge, attitudes and behaviour described by Green (1998) can perhaps be seen as extremes of more widespread social constructions of masculinity which result in 'normal' male sexual aggression against females (Kelly et al, 1992; Meyer, 1996), constructions which thrive in the contexts of prohibition, secrecy and adult discomfort in relation to children's sexuality and sexual development outlined above.

Thus, what emerges is that matters of childhood sexuality and development are highly complex and charged with emotion, prescription and proscription. Recognising the sexuality of children and young people may be problematic in itself, given notions of childhood innocence and asexuality, and working with children and young people whose behaviour has been deemed to be sexually abusive readily leads into much wider and contested debates about normal child sexual development and gender relationships – a veritable minefield of argument and uncertainty.

CHILDHOOD INNOCENCE AND CHILD SEXUALITY – LIVE ISSUES

A relatively recent article written by Birkett in the The Guardian weekend magazine (February 12 2000) and subsequent correspondence from the NSPCC provide an interesting illustration of the live nature of the debates which have been discussed thus far in this section. Birkett's article is entitled *The End of Innocence*, with the front page containing a painting of two cherubic-looking children. Interspersed amongst the text are further photographs of young boys either holding footballs or a teddy, one of the youngsters also wearing an 'alien' mask. After quoting NSPCC statistics about the amount of child abuse committed by other children, criminal statistics about young sexual offenders and media coverage of alleged sexual abuse by young children Birkett asks:

> *In this new, unsettling moral universe, is our children's normal sexual development being criminalised? Does touching your sister's genitals, once, become an abusive act? Is experimentation between children being unnecessarily seen as a mighty problem that needs to be tackled? Is an over-zealous interest in Postman's Knock really the signature of an apprentice paedophile? Is French kissing another six year old assault? Is 'show me yours and I'll show you mine' a sexually inappropriate request? Is the unimaginable really happening in the enchanted land? Is this the end of innocence?*(Birkett, 2000: p. 15)

Birkett describes at considerable length the case of a 10 year boy (whom she describes as a 'Lilliputian Sex Offender') accused of molesting a little girl with whom he played football, detailing the trauma experienced by the boy and his family occasioned by the subsequent court proceedings when he was eventually found guilty of an indecent assault. This story is written in a tone that suggests the way the case was handled was heavy handed and an instance of the criminalisation of normal horseplay or sexual experimentation. Other cases of alleged sexual abusers are detailed in a similar fashion.

Birkett goes on to report on an increasing number of (NSPCC) projects working with young sexual abusers in 'this new and burgeoning professional field', planned, she comments, 'to stop young abusers becoming the serial paedophiles in the future' (Birkett, 2000: 17). Then, after illustrating the uncertainties about our knowledge of child sexual development which have already been discussed, she expresses considerable doubt about the job of providing signposts through this:

murky emotional landscape ... (which is) being increasingly handed over to the young abuser professionals who decide what is acceptable and what is not. There's an understandable desire among these experts to get to grips with the grey area of nascent sexual development. They want to draw up some harder and faster rules.(Birkett, 2000: p. 19)

Thus, Birkett appears to be suggesting that a moral panic about what is essentially innocent child behaviour is being whipped up and driven by professionals wedded to a child protection orthodoxy which claims that, unless identified and treated, young sexual abusers will become the adult sex offenders of tomorrow, a discourse which has already been discussed. She concludes the article:

Once upon a time, we believed in and trusted our children. Can we ever return to this enchanted land? Can childhood be reclaimed? Or are our little angels forever branded little devils? ... We seem to have forgotten that we were once young, and lived in a messy emotional world, where we struggled to find out what we wanted to do and what we wanted to have done to us. We have forgotten what it is like to trespass gingerly into a place, that we hadn't yet charted, whose rules we hadn't yet learned - the world of grown-up sexuality.(Birkett, 2000: p. 20)

The NSPCC, whose projects were referred to and whose staff gave interviews to Birkett, was apparently so alarmed by the impression conveyed by the article that the Director of Public Policy put his name to a letter which appeared in *The Guardian* on February 14th, a letter which conveys a certainty which is perhaps not supported by existing literature on child sexual development. Thus what he wrote includes the following:

When working with the serious issue of abusive behaviour by children, the NSPCC's response is informed by our understanding of child development. In doing so we address these serious concerns without confusing them with normal, healthy child development ... Children involved in 'horseplay or 'kiss chase' or normal playground behaviour are not referred to us. Natural sexual curiosity and experimentation is a healthy part of growing up. In attempting to link this unrelated subject with serious sexual abuse by children, the article denigrates a very real problem ... It has taken all of us a long time to grasp that sexual abuse of children does happen. Now we need to grasp that sometimes children do this to children. (Noyes, 2000: p. 19)

Although there are some serious points made in Birkett's article, its tone and the language used are emotive and dramatic. It provides, it can be argued, a pertinent illustration of the application of the Appollonian construction of childhood discussed by Jenks (1996), with its repeated references to the innocence of children and its claim that the significance of some childhood behaviours is being misinterpreted. In contrast, the article contains a barely disguised attack on professionals who are portrayed as powerful experts who are redefining, on the basis of a rigid and flawed moral orthodoxy, the innocent activities of children who are consequently being traumatised and oppressed by child protection and court processes. As is discussed later in this section, perhaps an alternative construction of children as both innocent and capable of abusive behaviour would serve the needs of young sexual abusers better?

Thus far in this section the focus has been on how issues of concern and uncertainty in relation to children and young people who sexually abuse can be more fully understood with reference to social constructions of childhood (innocence) and to existing literature on child sexuality. Now the focus switches to a key issue for many professionals: how to dovetail the workings of child care/child protection and criminal justice systems in respect of young sexual abusers. What becomes clear is how changing opinions or perspectives about how children who break the law should be managed and whether they should be treated differently from other children in difficulty have had a major influence on the development of children's and criminal justice legislation during this century. In turn, this has had consequences for how easily or otherwise the problem of children and young people who sexually abuse might be addressed.

CRIMINAL YOUTH: DEPRIVED OR DEPRAVED?

In contrast to Jenks (1996), who claims that Appollonian conceptions are currently dominant, Hendrick (1994 and 1997) argues that notions of children as (unprotected, deprived) victims and as (delinquent, depraved) threats have actually co-existed uneasily for at least this century. He traces the history of legislation about children and youth crime since the 1908 Children Act which established juvenile courts separate from adult courts and which placed limits on the imprisonment of children, as reflecting rapidly fluctuating perceptions about how to deal with neglected and delinquent children, either together (because their needs are the same) or as separate categories of child (the deprived and the depraved). Muncie (1999a), making much the same point as Hendrick, goes on to identify four distinct but over-lapping strategies for dealing with young offenders – welfare-based, justice-based, diversionary and custodial interventions – and comments that studying the impact of these strategies on youth justice policy is:

predominantly a history of political and professional debate, in which diverse and competing discourses of welfare, justice, diversion and custody have come to do battle over their respective places in the management of the 'delinquent body'.(Muncie, 1999a: p. 254)

It is not the purpose of this overview to track this history in detail, the focus here is on certain, more recent aspects of this history which are helpful in illuminating possible reasons why those professionals responding to young sexual abusers over the age of criminal responsibility have struggled to develop coherent systems of response.

THE WELFARE DISCOURSE

Muncie (1999a) outlines how the period between the implementation of the 1908 Children Act and the 1970s saw the growing ascendancy of the welfare discourse: that children in trouble (the depraved), whose criminal behaviour was viewed as firmly linked to social, economic and physical disadvantage, were as much in need as neglected (deprived) children and that they required rehabilitation and re-integration into society, managed by a range of professionals. Muncie and many other commentators (see, for example, Hendrick, 1994; 1997; Anderson, 1999; Goldson, 1999; Tutt, 1999) have all argued that the Children and Young Person's Act 1969 (CYPA 1969) which was implemented in January 1971 was a particularly significant milestone in this welfarist approach to juvenile delinquency and children generally. Thus the Act was designed to increase the effectiveness of the measures available to combat juvenile delinquency via alternatives to detention, based on treatment, non-criminal care proceedings and care orders. Approved schools were to be abolished, compulsory removal of a child from his or her home was to take the form of a committal to the care of the local authority, supervision of all children under the age of 17 was to be by the local authority and new forms of treatment intermediate between long term residential and community provisions were envisaged. Included in the Act, too, was the provision to raise the age of criminal responsibility incrementally to 14 years of age.

Muncie (1999a) argues that as a result of the CYPA 1969 the primary duties of juvenile courts became those of care, protection and provision for all children, as opposed to making decisions about innocence or guilt within a criminal justice context based on individual responsibility and punishment. Moreover, social workers were to play a key role in making decisions about how delinquents should be treated. He comments:

Authority and discretion were notably shifted out of the hands of the police, magistrates and prison department and into the hands of local authorities and the Department of Health and Social Security. As Thorpe et al declared, 'the hour of the "child savers" had finally arrived (Thorpe et al, 1980, p.6).(Muncie, 1999a: p. 259)

Had the problem of children and young people who sexually abuse been 'discovered' at this time then it may well be that the task of developing policy and procedure in respect of this group might have been a great deal easier for professionals and agencies as the Act, thus, virtually obliterated any distinctions previously made between deprived and depraved children and gave local authorities the prime responsibility for young offenders. Similarly, the child protection discourse which has been described about how young sexual abusers should be managed, perhaps under a legal mandate and treated for their pathological behaviour, would have sat quite easily with the provisions contained in the Act.

However, whether the best interests of children and young people and their rights to natural justice would have been served is debatable because the 1970s, partly as an unintended consequence of the welfarist ideology just described, were characterised by substantial increases in children being removed to residential care and imprisoned in detention centres or borstals (Goldson 1997; 1999; Tutt, 1999). Ironically the CYPA 1969 was, also, always under attack from those who felt it was too permissive and the Conservative government elected in 1970 announced that it would not be raising the age of criminal responsibility or replacing criminal with care proceedings. Detention centres and attendance centres were never phased out and approved schools remained, though under the guise of a new title: community homes with education. Magistrates continued to punish traditional, usually older, male offenders within criminal proceedings with the welfarist ideology of the Act tending to be targeted on other groups: young women; chronic truants and others thought to be at risk.

Thus, during the 1970s the welfare strategy for dealing with juvenile delinquents came under increasing criticism. Muncie (1999a) suggests that this critique had three main and somewhat contradictory elements: commentators on the right were arguing that once again the system was being too soft on crime (despite the clear evidence noted above that increasing numbers of children and young people were being taken into care or imprisoned); strong attacks were being made on the arbitrary power of social workers to make decisions which greatly restricted the liberties of children whose crimes were often of a minor nature; and others were expressing concern about young people being denied their legal rights and due process in court.

THE JUSTICE IDEOLOGY

Thus, by the early 1980s, youth justice approaches had re-emerged, based on a justice ideology (Goldson 1997 and 1999; Tutt, 1999), which advocated equality before the law, the importance of due legal process and the need for determinate sentences based on the seriousness of an offence not on individual need. However, interestingly, the 1982 Criminal Justice Act which gave magistrates further powers to sentence people to youth custody, for example, also endorsed the expansion of schemes to divert juveniles from crime, prosecution and custody. Diversion was repeatedly affirmed in government documents (e.g. Home Office, 1980) consultative documents (Home Office, 1984) and the Code of Practice for Prosecutors (Crown Prosecution Service, 1986). It was made clear that prosecution should not occur unless it was absolutely necessary or as a last resort and that the prosecution of first-time offenders where the offence was not serious was unlikely to be justifiable unless there were exceptional circumstances. These principles were echoed in local police force procedures.

The result was that the proportion of 14-16 year olds cautioned for indictable offences increased from 34% in 1980 to 73% in 1992 and for 10-13 year old boys from 65% to 92%. Home Office Circular 14/1985 (Home Office, 1985) explicitly referred to the dangers of net-widening and encouraged the use of no further action or informal warnings instead of even formal cautions. In many police areas instant cautions were also introduced. Thus, between 1982 and the early 1990s there was a substantial decline both in the number of juveniles prosecuted and in the rate of known juvenile offending (DoH, 1994). The 1988 Criminal Justice Act, which introduced strict criteria before custody was to be considered, continued these trends, as did the 1991 Criminal Justice Act, which established a range of (Intermediate Treatment) community sentences within a broad philosophy of 'punishment in the community' (Muncie, 1999a).

McLaughlin and Muncie (1993) have charted how the role of social workers and social work departments in relation to youth crime changed correspondingly during this period. Agreeing with critiques of the welfare approach adopted by social workers previously, many social work departments, with Department of Health and Social Security encouragement, embraced the new justice and alternatives to custody models for young offenders which were being promulgated. Youth justice teams within social work departments, separate from teams involved with children in need of care and protection, were created based on policies of minimum intervention and maximum diversion. Thus, for example, Muncie (1999a) comments that:

social enquiry reports, were no longer constructed around the treatment model of delinquency and notions of family pathology, but focused more closely on the offence and the offender.(Muncie, 1999a: p. 283)

In addition, systems for interagency consultation involving youth justice staff, probation, other social services staff, education and the police became well established, where decisions were taken at the pre-court stage to maximise the potential for diversion (Davis et al, 1989).

Considerable success was, thus, being achieved by managing to keep most juveniles out of the system (Nellis, 1991), with custody reserved for the few deemed to be hardened criminals and high risk (a process often described as *bifurcation*).

The changes and central principles of the 1989 Children Act were also of significance. The care order was no longer available to the court in criminal proceedings and the offence condition was removed from care proceedings. The change recognised the decline in the use made of the order, youth justice arguments about its inappropriateness anyway in criminal proceedings, and popular principles of determinacy in sentencing and of parental responsibility, partnership, family support and voluntary agreements (Harris, 1991). New rules provided for the transfer of care proceedings from the juvenile court to the renamed family proceedings court, while the newly named youth court only dealt with criminal proceedings. Thus, a much clearer demarcation between the deprived young person in need of care and protection and the depraved youngster who had broken the law had re-emerged, with separate systems in place for the processing of youngsters deemed to fall within these respective categories.

It is hardly surprising then, when the problem of children and young people who sexually abused emerged in the early 1990s, that professionals would struggle to integrate a system for dealing with young offenders with another system responsible for children in need of care and protection, systems which had become increasingly demarcated from each other, not only in terms of personnel but also in terms of approach and philosophical underpinnings. Indeed, some commentators have looked back nostalgically on the older welfarist ideology of only a few years previously as providing a much more workable framework within which to develop responses to young sexual abusers. Thus, for example, the abolition of the criminal care order brought about by the Children Act 1989 was seen by some of those involved in the construction of the problem of young sexual abusers as an unfortunate consequence of the new legislation, Morrison, one time Chair of NOTA, commenting:

> *With regards to juvenile sex offenders, the main effect of the Act has been to end criminal care orders, at a point where some would argue, a real purpose has been found for them.*(Morrison et al, 1994: p. 37)

CHILDREN AND YOUNG PEOPLE WHO SEXUALLY ABUSE – DEPRAVED AND DEPRIVED?

In keeping with the rapidly changing fortunes of the various discourses around about how to deal with young people who break the law, justice based models for tackling youth crime have themselves been criticised by those with a more welfarist focus for neglecting the particular circumstances and needs of individual offenders (Muncie, 1999a). Indeed, as various commentators have argued (see, for example, Crisp, 1994; Hendrick, 1994 and 1997), whether children are perceived as innocent victims or uncontrollable threats, there are, in fact, few objective differences in their characters and needs. Boswell's (1995) study of violent and very disturbed young people detained under Section 53 orders of the Children and Young Persons Act 1933 (as amended by subsequent criminal justice legislation) for children convicted of offences for which an adult may be sentenced to 14 years' imprisonment or more, provides ample supportive evidence of these ideas. She clearly documents the prevalence of childhood abuse and/or loss within this group of youngsters and, indeed, she suggests that their subsequent violent behaviour can be seen as manifestation of post-traumatic stress disorder requiring counselling and support, not punishment. Similarly, despite societal preoccupations with the threat that James Bulger's killers presented, there was also clear, well publicised evidence that these were two unhappy and disturbed people, in need of nurturance, caring, protection *and* control.

In the same way, as the overview of available theory and research on the needs and characteristics of young sexual abusers outlined earlier appeared to indicate, children and young people who sexually abuse others can be disturbed and troubled children themselves. They may have been abused in their own childhood, they often come from problematic family situations, and they may lack social skills and be doing poorly in school, a constellation of factors which is also common in the backgrounds of other violent and non-violent youngsters (Beckett, 1999). Thus, in simplistic terms, they may be both deprived and depraved, and, hence, in need of services which can address both aspects. In this sense it would appear that they are little different from other young offenders, all of whom might benefit from more integrated approaches to their management. However, as Muncie comments:

> *The two philosophies of criminal justice and welfare remain incompatible, because while the former stresses full criminal responsibility, the latter stresses welfare and treatment to meet the needs of each individual child. The defining of what constitutes 'need' was, and remains problematic. Welfarism, it seems, is just as capable of drawing more young people into the net of juvenile justice as it is of affording them care and protection. Moreover the very existence of a system legitimised by 'welfare' is always likely to come under attack from those seeking more retributive and punitive responses to young offending.*(Muncie, 1999a: p. 257)

As will be discussed in the final section of this monograph, subsequent developments within youth justice and the child protection/child welfare systems during the later 1990s, which are resulting in a widening gap between child welfare and youth crime services are, in many ways, only serving to increase the complications for professionals and agencies trying to develop consistent and coherent services for children and young people who sexually abuse others.

CHAPTER 6
THE COMPLICATIONS INCREASE

The aim of this final chapter is to bring the reader up-to-date with changes in policy and legislation since the mid 1990s, all of which have impacts on policy, procedures and services for children and young people who sexually abuse. Thus, the complexities of responding to young sexual abusers which were theorised and analysed in the last section are further considered within the context of developments in youth justice and child care/child protection services, as well as new legislation in respect of adult sex offenders. These changes, which are overviewed in turn, comprise:

- the enactment of the 1998 Crime and Disorder Act;
- the 'refocusing debate' within child protection systems; and the revision of *Working Together* (DoH, 1991);
- increased public and political attention on adult sex offenders and the passing of the Sex Offenders Act, 1997, together with related provisions within the 1998 Crime and Disorder Act.

It will be argued that, whilst there are some positive aspects in these changes for developments in work with young sexual abusers, nevertheless, the overall picture has probably become even more complicated. In the concluding section of the chapter some pointers for good policy and practice are suggested.

DEVELOPMENTS IN APPROACHES TO YOUTH CRIME AND THE 1998 CRIME AND DISORDER ACT

In a previous sub-section the account of policy and legislative developments in relation to youth crime concluded with a brief reference to the Criminal Justice Act 1991 which Goldson (1997) and Muncie (1999a), for example, have argued was the final piece of a jigsaw of legislative measures passed during the previous decade which supported the 'justice' approach to youth crime, with its principles of diversion, decriminalisation and decarceration. However, hardly had that Act been passed than the public and political climate changed, with developments during 1993 in particular being seen by many commentators as something of a watershed in this process (Crisp, 1994; Goldson, 1994; 1997; Sone, 1994; Muncie, 1999a; Payne, 1999;). Thus, Goldson has commented:

> *... in 1993 – against what appeared to be a backdrop of political consensus regarding the legitimacy and efficacy of the 'justice' directed policy and practice – a reactionary U turn was launched which rapidly dismantled the successful practice orientation of the previous decade and set a harsh new tone in relation to state responses to children in trouble.*(Goldson, 1997: p. 79)

Similarly Muncie (1999a) has made the point that:

> *... the period 1991-3 may well go down in the chronicles of youth justice as yet another watershed when the public, media and political gaze fixed upon the perennial issue of juvenile crime and delivered a familiar series of knee-jerk and draconian measures.*
> (Muncie, 1999a: 286)

A MORE PUNISHMENT ORIENTED APPROACH TO YOUTH CRIME

Various factors have been credited with contributing to this tougher youth crime offensive. Firstly, there were the public and political reactions to the James Bulger murder in early 1993, albeit an exceptional case, which fed into growing but empirically unsupported media and public conceptions of increasing childhood lawlessness and Dionysian portrayals of children in trouble as evil and alien 'joy riders', 'ram raiders', 'bail bandits' and 'miscreants' (Crisp, 1994; Franklin and Petley, 1996; Muncie 1999a; Payne, 1999). Secondly, there was increasing pressure from the courts and others who thought that penal policy had become far too liberal. The courts, in particular, were not happy with the constraints placed on their sentencing powers by the Criminal Justice Act 1991 (Goldson, 1997). Finally, there was an embattled Conservative government desperate to improve its image with the public with its new morality and 'back to basics' rhetoric. Thus, Michael Howard, then Home Secretary, addressed the Conservative Party Conference in October 1993 and, to great applause, said, 'We are all sick and tired of young hooligans who terrorise communities' and promised that 'we will get on, pass legislation, build these centres and take these thugs off the streets' (Crisp, 1994; Goldson 1994; 1997; Anderson, 1999; Muncie, 1999a).

The consequence of this about-turn in public and political perceptions has been the passing of a series of Criminal Justice Acts during the 1990s which provide evidence of a much tougher, retributive, punishment oriented approach to youth crime, albeit with preventive strategies also included in recognition of growing evidence that such strategies appear to be effective in reducing youth crime (Audit Commission 1996 and 1998). Even these preventive measures, however, have become increasingly intrusive and stringent. Thus, the 1993 Criminal Justice Act seriously weakened the impact of the 1991 Criminal Justice Act by relaxing the criteria restricting the use of custodial sentences and the 1994 Criminal Justice and Public Order Act introduced, amongst other provisions, secure training centres for children as young as 12, a doubling of the maximum sentence of custody permitted within a young offender institution and American style 'boot camps' (Nathan, 1995).

Nor did this trend alter with the election of the first Labour government for 18 years in May 1997. As Shadow Home Secretary, Tony Blair had vowed to be 'tough on crime and tough on the causes of crime' in the 1997 Labour Party Manifesto and the youth justice provisions within the Labour Government's 1998 Crime and Disorder Act have been described by Muncie (1999b) as 'institutionalised intolerance', targeted not just at young offenders but at young people generally. Of fundamental significance within the Act is the abolition of *doli incapax*, which had existed in English law since the fourteenth century and which assumed that children might not appreciate the difference between right and wrong. Thus, a child between the ages of 10 and 14 convicted of a criminal offence had also to be shown to understand that what he or she had done was criminally wrong. The abolition of *doli incapax* has been seen by many commentators as confirmation of the UK's current punitive stance in relation to youth crime, a legislative move which also contravenes article 40 of the UN Convention on the Rights of the Child (see, for example, Bandalli, 1998; Muncie 1999b; Payne, 2000a).

The intentions of the 1998 Crime and Disorder Act were clearly expressed in the White Paper *No More Excuses* (Home Office 1997), published thirty years after the *Children in Trouble* White Paper of the 1960s (Home Office, 1968). The contents and language used in the latter White Paper supported the view that children in trouble in the community should not be treated differently from other deprived children, their behaviour being seen as resulting from social disadvantage. In contrast, *No More Excuses*, as its title suggests, was arguing that personal responsibility and accountability should inform youth justice approaches. As Tutt (1999) has pointed out even the language had changed from 'children' to 'youth' and 'young offenders'.

Thus, the White Paper *No More Excuses* (Home Office, 1997) recommended that a clear strategy was needed to prevent offending and reoffending; that offenders and their parents face up to their offending behaviour and its effects on families, victims and communities; that offenders take responsibility for their behaviour; that earlier, more effective intervention when young people first offend should be developed, with the aim of helping young people develop a sense of personal responsibility; that there should be faster, more efficient procedures from arrest to sentence; and that closer partnerships across youth justice agencies were needed to deliver an improved system.

The subsequent 1998 Crime and Disorder Act, which received royal assent in July 1998, therefore, signalled a return to a more interventionist, punitive and net-widening approach, particularly in terms of crime prevention work (Bell, 1999; Payne, 2000b). Thus, the Act includes child safety orders and child curfew orders which can target children even under the age of 10. Cautions are replaced by reprimands and final warnings, the latter having the potential to trigger services from the new Youth Offending Teams (see later).

The emphasis on accountability and personal responsibility made clear in the White Paper *No More Excuses* (Home Office, 1997) was also reflected in a range of new sentencing provisions within the Act including:

- re-sentencing for an original offence on breach of a supervision order and allowing courts a full range of sentencing disposals;
- reparation orders through which offenders are expected to undertake specific reparation to their victims, including a supervised meeting with the victim;
- action plan orders – short-term task focused orders;
- parenting orders which require parents to attend a number of specified sessions aimed at improving their parenting skills.

All in all then, policy and legislation in relation to youth crime since the late 1990s is dramatically different from what was in place when the problem of children and young people who sexually abuse first emerged in the early 1990s. Thus, as Muncie (1999b) has argued, current strategies for dealing with young offenders have shifted away from even traditional welfare and/or justice approaches to youth crime, towards new, harsher, net-widening and more managerial approaches to cost effective and efficient ways of dealing with the delinquent population which have the effect of providing a less humane service to young people. Ironically, in contrast, changes in approaches to child protection work during the mid to late 1990s have moved in a very different direction as will now be discussed, changes which also impact on policy, procedures and services for children and young people who sexually abuse.

REFOCUSING DEBATE IN CHILD PROTECTION WORK AND THE REVISION OF WORKING TOGETHER (DoH, 1991)

The 'refocusing debate' in child protection had its roots in the publication of *Messages from Research* (DoH, 1995) which summarised the key findings of 20 research studies, many of which were commissioned by the Department of Health through its child protection research programme. Amongst the conclusions reached by *Messages from Research* was the view that too many children and families were being unnecessarily caught up in the child protection process, causing stress to those families and alienation from services. Thus, research had indicated that over half of the children and families who were subject to section 47 enquiries received no services, enquiries being too narrowly focused on whether abuse or neglect had occurred rather than considering the wider needs and circumstances of the child and family

(Gibbons et al, 1995). On the other hand, some professionals, it appeared, were using section 47 enquiries inappropriately as a means of obtaining services for children in need. In similar vein, child protection case conferences were criticised for focusing too heavily on decisions about registration and removal, rather than focusing on the development of plans to support children and their families. The gradual process of net-widening in the child protection system was, it was being suggested, in need of reversal in order to divert families, not presenting significant risk of harm, out of the system so as to address their needs in a less invasive and less formalised manner.

CHILDREN IN NEED, NOT CHILDREN AT RISK

The key to this refocusing debate was a philosophical shift that would see such children as primarily 'children in need' under the Children Act, 1989 rather than 'children at risk'. The language had, thus, changed from 'risk' and 'protection' to 'need' and 'safety'. Relevant agencies, it was argued, should be promoting access to a range of services for children in need without inappropriately triggering child protection processes. Partnerships with children and families should be improved so that families were encouraged to reveal their problems and obtain the help they needed and skilled assessment by professionals, working across traditional agency boundaries, should be looking at children's developmental needs, parental capacity and wider family and environmental factors. Such assessments, it was being emphasised, should build on strengths, whilst also addressing difficulties.

Although the Department of Health published *Messages from Research* in 1995 there was then a hiatus in the sense that although revisions to *Working Together* (DoH, 1991) were promised to take on board this new philosophy, it took over four years for the new central government guidance document *Working Together to Safeguard Children* to be published (DoH, 1999). In the meantime agencies such as social services departments and ACPCs had to respond to the 'refocusing debate' as best they could. One of the authors of Masson and Morrison (1999) commented that, in his experience of working with ACPCs as a trainer and consultant, responses to the refocusing debate had:

> *resulted in an increased emphasis on diversionary approaches to reduce the numbers of children entering the child protection system.*(Masson and Morrison, 1999: p. 209)

Based on the perspective of the child protection discourse described earlier in the monograph, Masson and Morrison (1999) then went on to comment that such approaches might not serve the best interests of young sexual abusers in that the seriousness of their behaviour and their responsibility for it (as well as their needs) might continue to be best addressed through the invocation of child protection procedures.

REVISING WORKING TOGETHER (DoH, 1991) IN RELATION TO ABUSE BY CHILDREN AND YOUNG PEOPLE

Somewhat surprisingly, whilst the long-awaited consultation paper on revisions to the 1991 edition of *Working Together* (DoH, 1998) endorsed the need to avoid drawing families into the child protection system unnecessarily, in relation to abuse carried out by children and young people, it also confirmed that:

> *The Government continues to take the view that handling juvenile sexual abuse cases within ACPC procedures will continue to provide the most effective way of tackling the problem.*(DoH, 1998: Para 5.17)

However, paragraphs 5.17 and 5.18 of the consultation paper also invited discussion on if, and when, young sexual abusers should be subject to a child protection case conference or placed on a child protection register, although, the clear view was expressed that they should always be the subject of a written inter-agency plan. This provoked the following comment by Masson and Morrison (1999):

> *The latter suggestion could signal a loosening of the principle that young sexual abusers should be seen as children at risk of significant harm to sometimes being seen as 'children in need' under the Children Act 1989. What the wording certainly suggests is that professionals will be left to decide whether such cases should be managed through the child protection case conference process or diverted into some other form of inter-agency case planning process.*(Masson and Morrison, 1999: p. 209)

What the consultation document (DoH, 1998) also stated was the need for new guidance in order to address the inter-relationship between child protection and the new criminal justice processes for youth crime contained within the 1998 Crime and Disorder Act. In the context of concurrent developments in relation to youth crime this seemed very timely, although, in the consultation document itself there was no indication of what the contents of this guidance might include.

52 individuals and organisations responded to the 1998 DoH consultation document's questions about the circumstances in which alleged young abusers should be the subject of a child protection case conference and registered. Their responses contained the same range of views on these and other issues as found in the empirical research described earlier. Thus, 14 (26%) of the respondents argued that all young sexual abusers should be conferenced under child protection procedures, whereas, 13 (25%) thought that, as children in need, they should be the subject of a multi-agency strategy meeting rather than a child protection case conference. The remaining respondents did not made a clear statement on the issue.

On the subject of child protection registration 13 (25%) respondents thought that young sexual abusers should only be registered if they were themselves victims of abuse and nine respondents (17%) recommended the establishment of a separate DoH category for registering young sexual abusers. Eight respondents (15%) also emphasised the need for each young person to be the subject of a risk assessment and intervention plan and just two respondents (4%) specifically referred to the need to integrate child protection and youth justice systems of response.

PARAGRAPH 6.31-6.37 OF WORKING TOGETHER TO SAFEGUARD CHILDREN (DoH, 1999)

What was finally incorporated into the *Working Together to Safeguard Children* (DoH, 1999) is set out below:

Children and Young People Who abuse Others

6.31 Work with children and young people who abuse others – including those who sexually abuse/offend – should recognise that such children are likely to have considerable needs themselves, and also that they may pose a significant risk of harm to other children. Evidence suggests that children who abuse others may have suffered considerable disruption in their lives, been exposed to violence within the family, may have witnessed or been subject to physical or sexual abuse, have problems in their educational development, and may have committed other offences. Such children and young people are likely to be children in need, and some will in addition be suffering or at risk of significant harm, and may themselves be in need of protection.

6.32 Children and young people who abuse others should be held responsible for their abusive behaviour, whilst being identified and responded to in a way which meets their needs as well as protecting others. *Work with adult abusers has shown that many of them began committing abusing acts during childhood or adolescence, and that significant numbers have been subjected to abuse themselves. (my italics)* Early intervention with children and young people who abuse others, may therefore, play an important part in protecting the public by preventing the continuation or escalation of abusive behaviour.

6.33 Three key principles should guide work with children and young people who abuse others:

- there should be a co-ordinated approach on the part of youth justice and child welfare agencies;
- the needs of children and young people who abuse others should be considered separately from the needs of their victims; *and*
- an assessment should be carried out in each case, appreciating that these children may have considerable unmet developmental needs, as well as specific needs arising from their behaviour.

6.34 ACPCs and Youth Offending teams should ensure that there is a clear operational framework in place within which assessment, decision making and case management take place. Neither child welfare nor criminal justice agencies should embark upon a course of action that has implications for the other without appropriate consultation.

6.35 In assessing a child or young person who abuses another, relevant considerations include:

- the nature and extent of the abusive behaviours. In respect of sexual abuse, there are sometimes perceived to be difficulties in distinguishing between normal childhood sexual development and experimentation and sexually inappropriate or aggressive behaviour. Expert professional judgement may be needed, within the context of knowledge about normal child sexuality;
- the context of the abusive behaviours;
- the child's development, and family and social circumstances;
- needs for services, specifically focusing on the child's harmful behaviour as well as other significant needs; *and*
- the risks to self and others, including other children in the household, extended family or social network;

This risk is likely to be present unless: the opportunity to further abuse is ended, the young person has acknowledged the abusive behaviour and accepted responsibility and there is agreement by the young abuser and his/her family to work with relevant agencies to address the problem.

6.36 Decisions for local agencies (including the Crown Prosecution Service where relevant), according to the responsibilities of each, include:

- the most appropriate course of action within the criminal justice system, if the child is above the age of criminal responsibility;
- whether the young abuser should be subject of a child protection conference; *and*
- what plan of action should be put in place to address the needs of the young abuser, detailing the involvement of all relevant agencies.

6.37 A young abuser should be the subject of a child protection conference if he or she is considered personally to be at a risk of continuing significant harm. Where there is no reason to hold a child protection conference, there may still be a need for a multi-agency approach if the young abuser's needs are complex. Issues regarding suitable educational and accommodation arrangements often require skilled and careful consideration. (DoH, 1999: p. 70-71)

Although these paragraphs offer more detailed guidance than that contained in the 1991 edition of *Working Together* (DoH, 1991), it can be argued that various problems remain in respect of their contents. For instance, it may be assumed from the title that the guidance applies to all forms of abuse by children and young people, but much of the text focuses specifically on sexual abuse and draws on research from that field which is not necessarily so applicable. Moreover, the sentence italicised in paragraph 6.32 which had also been in the original paragraph 5.24 (DoH, 1991) does not properly reflect research findings in respect of recidivism rates of young sexual abusers (Beckett, 1999). There is also a lack of clarity about whether different arrangements should pertain to children under, as opposed to over, the age of criminal responsibility.

THE IMPLICATIONS OF RECENT CHANGES IN YOUTH CRIME AND CHILD WELFARE POLICY AND LEGISLATION ON CHILDREN AND YOUNG PEOPLE WHO SEXUALLY ABUSE

Looking, firstly, at some of the provisions of the 1998 Crime and Disorder Act, there are elements which fit reasonably comfortably with current treatment approaches to young people who commit sexual offences; for instance, the emphasis on responsibility, awareness of consequences for the victim and a new form of cautioning which can trigger service provision. In addition, one of the major consequences of the 1998 Crime and Disorder Act has been the creation, under Section 39 of the Act, of local Youth Offending Teams (YOTs), teams which were established during 1999-2001. These teams are responsible to a local authority's chief executive and comprise a manager, plus police, social work, probation, education and health staff. Together, their task is to prevent offending by children and young people (Home Office, 1997), drawing on the different skill bases of those involved including:

the child protection, public care and welfare expertise of social services; the assessment and supervisory role of the probation service with its knowledge of working with young offenders to change their behaviour; the community policing and crime prevention work of the police with an enhanced role for reparation and rehabilitation; the education department's links with truanting and excluded pupils and often unaddressed special educational needs; and the diagnosis and referral for substance misuse and mental health problems available from the health service.(Payne, 2000a)

In addition to the provision of direct services, YOTs are required to formulate a local youth justice plan, based on audits of the types and needs of young offenders, and services. The relevant Home Office guidance (1998b) specifically mentioned juvenile sex offenders amongst the type of offenders who can be included in this audit. The guidance also referred to the need to develop effective information systems to monitor the outcomes of intervention.

At a national level, a Youth Justice Board (an executive, non-departmental public body) has been established under Section 41 of the 1998 Crime and Disorder Act with a remit to:

- advise the Home Secretary on the operation of the youth justice system;

- establish national standards;
- maintain a rolling programme of inspections;
- approve local youth justice annual plans;
- initiate training;
- identify and disseminate good practice; and
- act as the commissioning and purchasing agent for the juvenile secure state.

Whilst the question of resources remains an issue in the further development of YOTs, the emphasis on auditing local need, combined with the establishment of the strategic national-level Board, do, it would appear, provide a possibility of developing a more coherent set of standards and practice in relation to juvenile sexual offenders. Indeed the initial efforts of the Youth Justice Board on various fronts are to be commended, including their joint funding of the mapping survey referred to earlier (Hackett, Masson and Phillips, in progress) and their funding of 6 development projects specifically working with young people who have sexually abused, for example, the AIM project in Greater Manchester which has close links with G-MAP. The AIM project was established in 1999, following a successful bid by 10 YOTs and other professionals in Greater Manchester for three year funding, which has now been extended. The project has established inter-agency policies and procedures for use in the locality (including negotiating extended police bail periods so initial assessments can be completed), provides training for practitioners and managers and has developed various models of assessment for use with the under 10s, adolescents, parents and carers and intellectually disabled young people, models which focus both on strengths in a young person's situation as well as areas of concern.

On the other hand, the increasingly tough approach to youth crime described earlier, together with a hardening of attitudes towards adult sex offenders which will be discussed later in this chapter, may, instead, result in more young people being found guilty of sexual offences. As a consequence, they may well receive custodial and other retributive sentences which will do little to address their offending behaviour nor any underlying social and/or emotional difficulties they may have (Littlechild and Masson, 2002).

Turning now to recent changes in child welfare and protection policy and guidance, and in summary, what is now in place in paragraphs 6.31-6.37 of *Working Together* (DOH, 1999) can be seen as an improvement on paragraph 5.24 of *Working Together* (DoH, 1991) particularly in the sense that some 'joined up thinking' is now recommended in respect of children over the age of criminal responsibility, however elusive the achievement of 'joined up' practice might be. Moreover, in that a child protection discourse in respect of children and young people who sexually abuse is still evident in the language used and content of paragraphs 6.31 – 6.37, as well the discourse of 'need', there is the potential for a meeting of minds between those coming from a child protection perspective and those from a youth crime background.

Notwithstanding, however, the potential benefits arising from the implementation of the 1998 Crime and Disorder Act and the somewhat extended and updated section in *Working Together to Safeguard Children* (DoH, 1999) it would appear, nevertheless, that young sexual abusers are now being managed in a context in which there are increasing ideological strains, at least at a national policy level, between interventionist youth crime approaches based on accountability and retribution and lower key welfare approaches based on the 'child in need' and partnership with families. Ironically, these are, in some ways, a reversal of the state of affairs pertaining to the period of the empirical research described in this report when justice approaches of diversion, decriminalisation and decarceration prevailed in approaches to young offenders and a more interventionist, child protection approach characterised much of the work of child care services.

Organisationally, too, the provision of services for 'deprived' children in need and 'depraved' young offenders seems to have become even more clearly demarcated than previously. The White Paper *No More Excuses* (Home Office 1997) had addressed the stereotypical view that 'welfarist' social services departments (and by implication the Department of Health) were not properly focused on the prime objective of work with young offenders – preventing offending – by effectively shifting responsibility for young offenders firmly to the Home Office, via the national Youth Justice Board and YOTs. Indeed, Tutt (1999) comments:

> *...the establishment of these teams has driven the final wedge between the youth justice system and the child care service. Although the **Quality Protects** programme, the government initiative for looked-after children, refers to reducing offending among looked-after children, there is increasing evidence of a widening gap between the processes for dealing with youth crime and the process for dealing with children in need.*(Tutt, 1999: p. viii)

ACPCs and YOTs, (two very different kinds of organisations anyway) and their constituencies are going to have considerable work to accomplish before integrated and coherent policies and procedures can be established. Some commentators (e.g. Calder 2002) are now arguing that the development of services for children and young people who have sexually abused has been put back ten years as a result of all these disconnected changes.

Given the existence of these increasingly divergent systems of response, a likely result will be the development of a double-track route so far as children and young people are concerned, with responses to themselves and their families, in effect, arbitrarily dependant on whether their cases happen to get referred to child care services or to the new youth crime service. This will have consequences not only for how their behaviour is regarded, but also for its management and the type of services that are considered appropriate. It may be that younger, less serious offenders will increasingly be responded to as children in need, with older, more serious offenders dealt with by youth crime services but, on the basis of existing research into the variable and inconsistent ways in which referrals were being dealt with in the early to mid 1990s, achieving this level of consistency will not be easy. Anyway, as discussed earlier, in common with many other types of young offenders, older, serious sexual offenders may also be very needy and socially disadvantaged. It remains to be seen if YOTs can develop services which address these needs as well as delivering on more punishment oriented government and public expectations.

Anecdotal evidence provides some support for the concern expressed in the last paragraph. In May 1999 the author was asked to make a presentation on policy and procedural issues in relation to children and young people who sexually abuse at the launch of a treatment project, joint funded by the local social services department and a national voluntary agency, which was offering assessment and treatment services to children and young people up to the age of 16 years who had sexually abused but who were not on court orders. Approximately 45 professionals attended the launch, from social services, voluntary agencies, the education department, the police and including substantial representation from the local youth justice service.

In the discussion time after the author's presentation virtually all the questions were from the youth justice staff who were expressing frustration about the lack of services which young sexual abusers on their caseloads were receiving. The youth justice staff explained that they only had time to complete social enquiry reports and make recommendations about sentence but they considered that many of these youngsters had a number of social and emotional needs which were not being met. What about comprehensive assessments and treatment for the youngsters they were working with? What should youth justice staff do when there were child protection issues which needed addressing? Who could they refer to? The local social services department child protection co-ordinator, who was also at the launch, said that social services area teams should pick up such referrals but he readily acknowledged that, due to staff shortages, they might well be resistant to doing so. It may be that the creation of YOTs will address these kinds of demarcation problems but clearly in this local area at least, a double-track route seemed very much in existence.

Based on telephone interviews conducted in 1999 with some of the professionals on the NCH Committee of Enquiry (NCH, 1992) similar concerns about the current arrangements seemed to be in evidence. Thus, in an interview with one of the committee members, children and young people who sexually abuse were described as 'dual status offenders', by which was meant child offenders who were also children in need. The interviewee considered that their dual status was not being addressed and that the 'present administration' was defensive and not willing to look at the issues involved. It was not thought that this lack of willingness to look at the issues was to do with 'get tough' policies as regards youth crime. Rather, it was conjectured that it demonstrated ministers' inability and unwillingness to cope with the complexity of dual status offenders.

Another of the NCH committee members interviewed agreed with the notion that children and young people who sexually abuse were children in need but felt they were being 'demonised' and locked into the criminal justice system (often in the adult court), inappropriately. Her opinion was that youth crime approaches, particularly since the introduction of the 1998 Crime and Disorder Act and the 1997 Sex Offenders Act (which is discussed shortly), were unhelpful, or that, at least, their implications for young sexual abusers had not been thought through.

A third committee member interviewee, commenting on the child protection narrative within the text of the NCH report (NCH, 1992), commented 'but it hasn't stuck has it?' When asked to clarify this statement it was suggested by the interviewee that the Home Office had never been willing to look at such youngsters as a separate category of children in trouble 'despite advice to do so.' The comment was made that the 1997 Sex Offenders legislation had been rushed through and the Home Office had not been able to respond to the consultation feedback about the complexity of issues in relation to young child abusers. Because it was too complex, it was suggested? The interviewee thought it was that and also because it was politically unacceptable to do so – 'the climate was against it'.

Most recently, however, a joint Chief Inspectors' Report on the arrangements for safeguarding Children (DoH, 2002) has specifically recommended that greater efforts need to be made so that YOTs address the welfare needs of young offenders. In addition the report recommends that every YOT should be a member of its local ACPC. Thus, there appears to be a beginning recognition, at central government level, that current systems of response to child welfare and protection issues and youth crime require better integration, to ensure that a holistic consideration of a given child and young person is achieved.

THE SEX OFFENDERS ACT 1997 AND RELATED PROVISIONS WITHIN THE 1998 CRIME AND DISORDER ACT AND THEIR IMPLICATIONS FOR YOUNG SEXUAL ABUSERS

Thus far, discussion has concentrated on the impact of major policy and legislative changes in youth justice and child protection/child welfare services on the problem of children and young people who sexually abuse. In addition, however, developing responses to this group have also been affected by a particular hardening of attitudes towards adult sex offenders.

What has become a major feature of the latter half of the 1990's is the intense focusing of attention, publicly and politically, on those who abuse, in a fashion which seems to exemplify the description of a moral panic and a concomitant role for 'paedophiles' as folk devils (Cohen, 1973).

Tracking of media coverage does not seem to suggest that similar attitudes are in evidence in respect of young sexual abusers. Indeed, the analysis of Birkett's article (Birkett, 2000) earlier seems to suggest quite the opposite. However, youngsters over the age of criminal responsibility are, nevertheless, subject to the 1997 Sex Offenders Act, the aim of which is to increase the ability of criminal justice agencies to monitor and share information on sexual offenders and, by doing so, to develop more effective risk management plans in order to prevent re-offending. The Act is based on the premise of the high risk of recidivism in adult sex offenders and in some cases the Act has already resulted in the use of intensive surveillance and other methods to prevent the offender having access to potential victims. Additional provisions within the 1998 Crime and Disorder Act have much the same aims.

The 1997 Sex Offenders Act places a requirement on all those adults and juveniles, convicted or cautioned for certain sexual offences, to register with the police within 14 days:

- their names and any other names they use;
- their address and subsequently any change of address;
- their date of birth.

The Act applies to all those convicted or cautioned from the date of its implementation and to all those who, at that point, were under the supervision of criminal justice agencies, or in custody for a specified sexual offence. The length of registration depends on the nature of the original sentence, varying from five years for a caution, to life for sentences of 30 months or more, or if committed to hospital under a restriction order. Overall, taking the 1997 crime statistics (Home Office, 1998a), had the Act been implemented then it would have resulted in approximately 1100 young people between 10 and 17 cautioned for sexual offences and 400 who were convicted, being registered.

The only distinction made for juvenile offenders is that their registration periods are half the length of those aged over 18 years and there is a duty of notification on their parent or guardian. Masson and Morrison (1999) have commented on the need for further consideration about the application of the Act to juveniles. For example, wide geographical variations in cautioning and prosecution practice (Evans and Wilkinson, 1990) are likely to result in very inconsistent patterns of registration.

The Act also enables, but does not require, the police to disclose their information to third parties, mainly other professionals in criminal justice and child protection settings, but also potentially to members of the public. This provision for disclosure is linked to the police making a risk assessment to determine when, and to whom, any disclosure will be made. In many authorities, the process of disclosure has been formalised through inter-agency protocols providing for the convening of risk management panels, either by the police or probation services or sometimes social services departments.

Masson and Morrison (1999) have pointed out that, in the case of juveniles, the likely response of parents to these registration requirements, and potentially to any suggestion that there might be public disclosure, will be critical. By way of illustration they described how:

In one case the family of a 15 year old boy in a group work programme was subject to an attempted arson attack on their home when neighbours discovered what he had done and the family eventually had to move out of the neighbourhood. If the registration system serves to increase the apprehensions and resistance of parents to engage in treatment work because they feel it is they, as much as their child, who are being 'blamed', then the Act's potential gains will have been more than outweighed by the alienation of the group most critical to the monitoring and management of juvenile offenders, their parents. This is not to suggest that registration is inappropriate for some juveniles, but that such decisions should be made on a case by case basis, through a process of multi-disciplinary decision-making.(Masson and Morrison, 1999: p. 212)

Clause 2 of the 1998 Crime and Disorder Act also makes provision for the police to seek sex offender orders on convicted sex offenders whose behaviour demonstrates a *risk* of re-offending and to obtain a civil injunction to monitor and restrain the offender's movements. In addition, provision is made for extended sentences to be imposed on sexually violent offenders. Although these last two sex offender provisions are aimed at adults, they nevertheless have the potential to affect juvenile sexual offenders.

The Sex Offenders Act and the relevant provisions of the 1998 Crime and Disorder Act, and their lack of flexibility in the case of juveniles, demonstrate the way in which interventionist philosophies and research about adult sex offenders are permeating criminal justice approaches to juveniles. In doing so these pieces of legislation fail to recognise that juvenile offenders are also 'children in need' under the 1989 Children Act, not just offenders and, in many cases, are also victims of harm themselves. Professionals here and in North America (Brown, 1998; ATSA, 1997) have also become concerned that assumptions about adult recidivism are being used to guide legislative policy with juvenile offenders. The workings of the 1997 Sex Offenders Act and of clause 2 of the 1998 Crime and Disorder Act with regard to juveniles may well increase the professional tensions identified earlier between youth crime and more welfarist child care philosophies of intervention. On the other hand some hope may be placed in the possibility of legislative reform in relation to sexual offences which takes into account the very particular needs of different ages of young sex offenders – 10-14 year olds, 14-17 year olds and 17-25 year olds, following the recent consultation exercise entitled *Setting the Boundaries: Reforming the Law on Sex Offences* (Home Office, 2000a).

CONCLUSION – SOME SUGGESTIONS FOR GOOD POLICY AND PRACTICE

Chapter 6 of this monograph has sought to demonstrate that increasingly divergent policy, legislative and organisational arrangements in respect of youth crime, child protection/child welfare work and adult sex offenders since the mid 1990s are probably serving to increase the complexities of work with children and young people who sexually abuse others. This is all the more problematic given that the empirical research outlined earlier has shown that professionals and agencies have been struggling to develop coherent and consistent policy, procedure and services for young sexual abusers for much of the last decade already, with only limited success. Whilst, as has been discussed, there may be various positives in some of the new arrangements which professionals may be able to make constructive use of, nevertheless, only time and further research (see, for example, Hackett, Masson and Phillips, in progress) will tell whether these complexities can be successfully addressed.

So what suggestions for good policy and practice seem relevant in this context? Looking at things from the perspective of local practitioners and managers, it would seem crucial that a multi-agency, co-ordinated approach is needed which, in the case of youngsters over 10 years of age, integrates child welfare/protection and youth crime systems of response. This will involve local ACPCs entering into a dialogue with their local YOT and other agencies in, for example, health and education, in order to develop local inter-agency policy and guidance which builds on the skeleton guidance in *Working Together* (DoH, 1999).

In progressing such inter-agency guidance, and in developing associated services, there is an increasing home-grown literature on which to draw. Erooga and Masson (1999) and Calder (2002), both of which comprise edited volumes with contributions from mainly UK contributors who are specialists in this field, may well prove to be of assistance. Two other recent publications also provide similar, relevant material on issues of case management and inter-agency co-ordination:

- *Childhood Lost* (The Bridge Consultancy, 2001) – a Part 8 Review (now called a serious case review) of the case of Dominic McGilligan, an 18-year-old with a history of sexual offending who had just left residential care when he raped and murdered an 11-year old boy in 1998;

- *I think I might need some more help with this problem* (Lovell, 2002) – an NSPCC report and recommendations on responding to children and young people who have sexually abused.

Investing in the consultative services of, for example, the Greater Manchester-based AIM project, mentioned earlier, may also prove to be money well spent. There is no point in re-inventing the wheel when such projects have already negotiated the tensions and dilemmas thrown up by national policy and legislation which are characterised by tensions and contradictions.

In developing a service for children and young people who sexually abuse, it is crucial to bear in mind that, although the majority of known young sexual abusers are adolescent males, the population comprises various groupings such as adolescent female abusers, young children who are exhibiting sexually provocative behaviours and children and young people with a learning disability. The local inter-agency network should, therefore, work to identify or create services which meet the various needs of this broad population. It is also important to bear in mind that only some young sexual abusers are at high risk of continuing their abusive behaviour. Thus, assessment processes and frameworks should be employed which try and identify these youngsters, so their welfare (both in terms of needs and controls) can be addressed and so the safety of others can be protected. Producing a framework which combines the holistic, needs-led framework published by the DoH (2000) with the more offence-specific focus of the ASSET framework (Home Office, 2000b) used by YOTs would seem a goal at which to aim in this context.

As regards interventions, it should not be assumed that models of work developed in relation to adult sex offenders are easily transferable, although elements are clearly relevant (see earlier in this monograph). Work with children and young people who sexually abuse should attend to their changing chronological and developmental needs and is likely to include personalised packages which might draw on one-to-one work, group-work and/or family-based interventions. Social skills training, sex education, counselling or therapy, courses in anger management, to name but a few approaches, may all usefully contribute to such packages. Some youngsters and their carers may benefit from only brief, purposeful contact with a relevant service; others, including those who are more disturbed and possibly at greater risk of re-abusing, may require much more long term support and intervention.

A small number of young sexual abusers may need to be placed away from their home environment because of the ongoing risk they present to other children, at home or in the community, or because of the risk they face staying where they are. The local inter-agency network will, therefore, need to consider if there is suitable alternative placement provision available within their locality and, if not, what placement provision should be developed to cater for their needs. It may be that co-operation across ACPC boundaries, combining scarce resources, would be appropriate in this situation, given the relatively small numbers needing such provision.

In progressing the development of policy, procedures and services for children and young people who sexually abuse, other issues should also be addressed, including the training and supervision of staff and professional carers; monitoring of local need; and the evaluation and review of what is put in place. Primary prevention work, for example, sex education and education about relationships in schools might also be considered as a useful investment, in order to reduce the numbers of young people who develop sexually inappropriate or abusive behaviours.

As will be obvious, none of the above will be achieved without the investment of professional time and the identification of resources, for example, to staff new service developments, provide training and supervision, and monitor and review service delivery. In the mid 1990s, lack of available resources were clearly an issue for many managers, some of whom, perhaps as a result, appeared reluctant to acknowledge that the problem of children and young people existed at all. Now, in the early 21st century, denial and minimisation of the problem does not appear to be an issue, at least within the professional community. Whether, however, in the next decade comprehensive and well integrated services for children and young people who sexually abuse are established across the country remains to be seen.

APPENDIX 1

5.24   ABUSE CARRIED OUT BY CHILDREN AND YOUNG PEOPLE

5.24.1   When abuse of a child is alleged to have been carried out by another child or young person, it is important that the appropriate child protection procedures should be followed in respect of both the victim and the alleged abuser.

5.24.2   Work with adult abusers has shown that many of them begin committing their abusing acts during childhood or adolescence, and further has indicated that significant numbers have suffered from abusing acts themselves. It is therefore an important child protection function to ensure that such behaviour is treated seriously and is always subject to a referral to child protection agencies. Such adolescent abusers are themselves in need of services.

5.24.3   Upon receipt of such referral there should be a child protection conference in respect of the alleged abuser to address current knowledge of:
- the alleged abuser
- their family circumstances
- the offence committed
- the level of understanding he or she has of the offence
- the need for further work.

This should include consideration of possible arrangements for accommodation, education (where applicable) and super-vision in the short term pending the compilation of a comprehensive assessment. This assessment should ideally involve a child psychiatrist to look at issues of risk and treatment.

5.24.4   Membership and handling of the conference, including initial plans, should be as prescribed in the standard child protection conference.

5.34.5   The conference should re-convene following the completion of the comprehensive assessment, to review the plan in light of the information obtained and to co-ordinate the interventions designed to dissuade the abuser from committing further abusive acts. Experience suggests that in many cases, policies of minimal intervention are not as effective as focused forms of therapeutic intervention which may be under orders of the civil or criminal courts.

(DoH, 1991: 37, paragraph 5.24)

REFERENCES

Abel, G., Becker, J., Cunningham-Rathner, J. and Rouleau, J. (1987) 'Self Reported Sex Crimes of 561 Non-incarcerated Paraphiliacs' in *Journal of Interpersonal Violence* 2 (6), p. 3–25

Ageton, S. (1983) *Sexual Assault among Adolescents*, MA, Lexington Books, Lexington

Ambert, A-M. (1995) 'Towards a Theory of Peer Abuse' in Ambert, A. M. (ed) *Sociological Studies of Children* (7), p.177–205

Anderson, B. (1999) 'Youth Crime and the Politics of Prevention' in Goldson, B. (ed) *Youth Justice: Contemporary Policy and Practice* Ashgate, London

Aries, P. (1962) *Centuries of Childhood* Jonathon Cape, London

Armstrong, H. (1995) *Annual Reports of Area Child Protection Committees 1993/1994* DoH, London

Armstrong, H. (1996) *Annual Reports of Area Child Protection Committees 1994/5* DoH, London

Armstrong, H. (1997) *Annual Reports of Area Child Protection Committees 1995/6* DoH, London

ATSA (1997) *Position on the Effective Legal Management of Juvenile Sexual Offenders* ATSA, Suite 26, Beaverton, Oregon

Audit Commission (1996) *Misspent Youth: Young People and Crime* Audit Commission, London

Audit Commission (1998) *Misspent Youth '98: The Challenge for Youth Justice* Audit Commission, London

Awad, G. and Saunders, E. (1989) 'Male Adolescent Sexual Assaulters' in *Journal of Interpersonal Violence* 6, p.446–60

Awad, G., Saunders, E. and Levene, J. (1984) 'A Clinical Study of Male Adolescent Sex Offenders' in *International Journal of Offender Therapy and Comparative Criminology* 28, p.105–116

Bandalli, S. (1998) 'Abolition of the Presumption of Doli Incapax and the Criminalisation of Children' in *The Howard Journal* 37, (2) p.114–123

Barbaree, H. E., Marshall, W. L. and Hudson, S. M. (eds) (1993) *The Juvenile Sex Offender* Guildford Press, London

Barker, M. and Morgan, R. (1993) *Sex Offenders: a Framework for the Evaluation of Community Based Treatment* Home Office, London

Baxter, D., Marshall, W., Barbaree, H., Davidson, P. and Malcolm, P. (1984) 'Differentiating Sex Offenders by Criminal and Personal History, Psychometric Measures and Sexual Response' in *Criminal Justice and Behaviour* 11, p.477–501

Becker, J. (1988) cited in Bentovim, A. and Williams, B. (1998) 'Children and Adolescents: Victims who Become Perpetrators' in *Advances in Psychiatric Treatment* 4, p.101–7

Becker, J. (1998) 'What We Know About the Characteristics and Treatment of Adolescents who have Committed Sexual Offenses' in *Child Maltreatment* 3(4), p.317–329

Beckett, R. (1999) Evaluation of Adolescent Sexual Abusers, in Erooga, M. and Masson, H. (eds) *Children and Young People who Sexually Abuse Others: Challenges and Responses* Routledge, London

Beckett, R., Beech, A., Fisher, D. and Fordham, S. (1994) *Community-based Treatment for Sex Offenders: An Evaluation of Seven Treatment Programmes* Home Office, London

Bell, C. (1999) 'Appealing for Justice for Children and Young People: A Critical Analysis of the Crime and Disorder Bill 1998' in Goldson, B. (ed) *Youth Justice: Contemporary Policy and Practice* Ashgate, London

Bentovim, A., Elton, A., Hildebrand, J., Tranter, M. and Vizard, E. (eds) (1988) Child Sexual Abuse in the Family and Related Papers, Wright, London

Birkett, D. (2000) The End of Innocence, in *The Guardian* Weekend magazine, February 12th, p.12–20

Bischof, G., Stith, S. and Whitney, M. (1995) 'Family Environments of Adolescent Sex Offenders and other Juvenile Delinquents' in *Adolescence* 30 (117), p.157–170

Blues, A., Moffatt, C. and Telford, P. (1999) 'Work with Adolescent Females who Sexually Abuse - Similarities and Differences' in Erooga, M. and Masson, H. (eds) *Children and Young People who Sexually Abuse Others: Challenges and Responses* Routledge, London

Blyth, E. and Cooper, H. (1999) 'Schools and Child Protection' in *Children, Child Abuse and Child Protection: Placing Children Centrally* The Violence against Children Study Group, Wiley, Chichester

Boswell, G. (1995) *Violent Victims* The Prince's Trust, London

Bradford, J., Bloomberg, D. and Bourget, D. (1988) 'The Heterogeneity/homogeneity of paedophilia' in *Psychiatric Journal of the University of Ottawa* 13, p.217–226

Brown, A. (1998) 'The Sex Offenders Act Part 1: Issues Relating to Adolescents Convicted of a Sexual Offence' in *NOTANews* 27, p.21–27

Brown, A. (1999) 'Working with Young People: Policy and Practice' in Erooga, M. and Masson, H. (eds) *Children and Young People who Sexually Abuse Others: Challenges and Responses* Routledge, London

Burton, D. L., Nesmith, A. A. and Badten, L. (1997) 'Clinician's Views on Sexually Aggressive Children and their Families: A Theoretical Exploration' in *Child Abuse and Neglect* 21(2), p.157–170

Butler, L. and Elliott, C. (1999) 'Stop and Think: Changing Sexually Aggressive Behaviour in Young Children' in Erooga, M. and Masson, H. (eds) *Children and Young People who Sexually Abuse Others: Challenges and Responses* Routledge, London

Calder, M. (ed) (2002) *Young People who Sexually Abuse. Building the Evidence Base for your Practice* Russell House Publishing, Lyme Regis

Cawson, P., Wattam, C., Brooker, S. and Kelly, G. (2000) *Child Maltreatment in the United Kingdom. A Study of the Prevalence of Child Abuse and Neglect* NSPCC, London

Chaffin, M. and Bonner, B. (1998) ' "Don't Shoot, We're Your Children" Have We Gone too Far in Our Response to Adolescent Sexual Abusers and Children with Sexual Behavior Problems' in *Child Maltreatment* 3 (4), p.314–316

Cicourel, A. V. (1967) *The Social Organisation of Juvenile Justice* Wiley, London

Cohen, S. (1973) *Folk Devils and Moral Panics: The Creation of Mods and Rockers* Paladin, London

Conte, J. (1985) 'Clinical Dimensions of Adult Sexual Abuse of Children' in *Behavioural Sciences and the Law* 3, p.341–354

Corby, B. (1993) *Child Abuse. Towards a Knowledge Base* Open University Press, Buckingham

Corby, B. (1998) *Managing Child Sexual Abuse Cases* Jessica Kingsley Publishers, London

Corby, B. (2000) *Child Abuse. Towards a Knowledge Base* 2nd Edn, Open University Press, Buckingham

Crisp A (1994) 'Children First' in *Community Care* Inside Youth Crime, 28 July–3 August, p.2–3

Crown Prosecution Service (1986), Code of Practice for Prosecutors, CPS, London

Davis, G., Boucherat, J. and Watson, D. (1989) 'Pre-court Decision Making in Juvenile Justice' in *British Journal of Criminology* 29(3), p.219–234

Department for Education (1994) 'Bullying: Don't Suffer in Silence. An Anti-bullying Pack for Schools' Department for Education, London

Department for Education and Employment (1995) Protecting *Children from Abuse: The Role of the Education Service* Draft Circular 10/95, Department for Education and Employment, London

DoH (1991) *Working Together Under the Children Act 1989 - A Guide to Arrangements for Interagency Co-operation for the Protection of Children from Abuse* HMSO, London

DoH (1994) *Social Focus on Children* HMSO, London

DoH (1995) *Messages from Research* HMSO, London

DoH (1998) *Working Together to Safeguard Children: New Government Proposals for Inter-agency Collaboration: Consultation Paper* DoH, London

DoH (1999) *Working Together to Safeguard Children: A Guide to Inter-agency Working to Safeguard and Promote the Welfare of Children* The Stationery Office, London

DoH (2000) *Framework for the Assessment of Children in Need and their Families* DoH, London

Dutt, R. and Phillips, M. (1996) 'Race Culture and the Prevention of Child Abuse, Background Paper 4 by the Race Equality Unit' in *Report of the National Commission of Inquiry into the Prevention of Child Abuse, Childhood Matters* The Stationery Office, London

Erooga, M. and Masson, H. (eds) (1999) *Children and Young People who Sexually Abuse Others: Challenges and Responses* Routledge, London

Evans, R. and Wilkinson, C. (1990) 'Variations in Police Cautioning Policy and Practice in England and Wales' in *Howard Journal* 29 (3), p.155–176

Farmer, E. and Pollock, S. (1998) *Sexually Abused and Abusing Children in Substitute Care* Wiley, Chichester

Featherstone, B. and Lancaster, E. (1997) 'Contemplating the Unthinkable: Men who Sexually Abuse' in *Critical Social Policy* 17 (4), p.51–71

Fehrenbach, P. A., Smith, W., Monastersky, C. and Deisher, R. W. (1986) 'Adolescent Sexual Offenders: Offender and Offence Characteristics' in *American Journal of Orthopsychiatry* 56, p.225–33

Fineran, S. and Bennett, L. (1998) 'Teenage Peer Sexual Harassment: Implications for Social Work Practice in Education' in *Social Work*,43 (1), p.55–64

Finkelhor, D. (1979) *Sexually Victimised Children* Free Press, New York

Finkelhor, D. (1984) *Child Sexual Abuse: New Theory and Research* Free Press, New York

Fisher, D. (1994) 'Adult Sex Offenders: Who are they? Why and How do they do it?' in Morrison, T., Erooga, M. and Beckett, R. (eds) *Sexual Offending against Children. Assessment and Treatment of Male Abusers* Routledge, London

Ford, M. and Linney, J. (1995) 'Comparative Analysis of Juvenile Sexual Offenders, Violent Nonsexual Offenders and Status Offenders' in *Journal of Interpersonal Violence* 10 (1), p.56–70

Foucault, M. (1979) *The History of Sexuality, Volume 1: An Introduction* Allen Lane, London

Franklin, B. and Horwath, J. (1996) 'The Media Abuse of Children' in *Child Abuse Review* 5, p.310–318

Franklin, B. and Petley, J. (1996) 'Killing the Age of Innocence: Newspaper Reporting of the Death of James Bulger' in Pilcher, J. and Wagg, S. (eds) *Thatcher's Children? Politics, Childhood and Society in the 1980s and 1990s* Falmer Press, London

Freeman-Longo, R., Bird, S., Stevenson, W. and Fiske, J. (1995) *1994 Nationwide Survey of Treatment Programs and Models: Serving Abuse Reactive Children, Adolescent and Adult Sex Offenders* Safer Society Press, Brandon, VT

Freud, S. (1978) 'Infantile Sexuality' in Strachey, J. (Ed. And Trans.) *The Standard Edition of the Collected Psychological Works of Sigmund Freud, Volume 7* Hogarth (original work published 1905), London

Fromuth, M. E., Jones, C. W. and Burkhart, B. R. (1991) 'Hidden Child Molestation: An Investigation of Perpetrators in a Non-clinical Sample' in *Journal of Interpersonal Violence* 6 (3), p.376–384

Furniss, T. (1983) 'Family Process in the Treatment of Intra-familial Child Sexual Abuse' in *Journal of Family Therapy* 5, p.263–278

Giaretto, H. (1981) 'A Comprehensive Child Sexual Abuse Treatment Program' in Mrazek, P. and Kempe, C. (eds) *Sexually Abused Children and their Families* Pergamon Press, New York

Gelles, R. (1997) *Intimate Violence in Families* 3rd edition, Sage, London

Gibbens, T., Soothill, K. and Way, G. (1981) 'Sex Offences against Young Girls: A Long Term Record Study' in *Psychological Medicine* 11, p.351–357

Gibbons, J., Conroy, S. and Bell, C. (1995) *Operating the Child Protection System: A Study of Child Protection Practices in English Local Authorities* HMSO, London

Glaser, D. and Frosh, S. (1988) *Child Sexual Abuse* Macmillan, London

Glasgow, D. (24.6.99), personal communication

Glasgow, D., Horne, L., Calam, R. and Cox, A. (1994) 'Evidence, Incidence, Gender and Age in Sexual Abuse of Children Perpetrated by Children: towards a Developmental Analysis of Child Sexual Abuse' in *Child Abuse Review* 3, p.196–210

Goldman, R. and Goldman, J. (1988) *Show me Yours: What Children Think about Sex* Penguin Books, London

Goldson, B. (1994) 'The Changing Face of Youth Justice' in *ChildRight* 105, p.5–6

Goldson, B. (1997) 'Children, Crime, Policy and Practice: Neither Welfare nor Justice' in *Children and Society* 11, p.77–88

Goldson, B. (ed) 1999 *Youth Justice: Contemporary Policy and Practice* Ashgate, London

Green, L. (1998) *Caged by Force, Entrapped by Discourse* PhD Thesis, University of Huddersfield

Groth, A. N. (1979) *Men Who Rape: The Psychology of the Offender* Plenum, New York

Grubin, D. (1998) *Sex Offending against Children: Understanding the Risk, Police and Reducing Crime Unit: Police Research Series Paper 99* Home Office, London

Hackett, S. (2000) 'Sexual Aggression, Diversity and the Challenge of Anti–oppressive Practice' in *The Journal of Sexual Aggression* 5 (1), p.4–20

Hackett, S., Masson, H. and Phillips, S. *Mapping and Exploring Services for young People who Sexually Abuse* funded by NOTA, NSPCC and YJB (in Progress)

Hallett, C. and Birchall, E. (1992) *Co-ordination and Child Protection. A Review of the Literature* HMSO, London

Hanks, H. (1994) ' "Normal" Psycho-sexual Development, Behaviour and Knowledge' in Calder, M. *Juveniles and Children who Sexually Abuse: A Guide to Risk Assessment* Russell House Publishing, Lyme Regis

Harris, R. (1991) 'The Life and Death of the Care Order (Criminal)' in *British Journal of Social Work* 21 (1), p.1–17

Hendrick, H. (1994) *Child Welfare England 1872-1989* Routledge, London

Hendrick, H. (1997) *Children, Childhood and English Society 1880-1990* Cambridge University Press, Cambridge

Hird, J. and Morrison, T. (1996) 'Six Groupwork Interventions with Adolescent Sexual Abusers' in *The Journal of Sexual Aggression* 2(1), p.49–63

HM Inspectorate of Probation (1998) *Exercising Constant Vigilance: The Role of the Probation Service in Protecting the Public from Sex Offenders* Home Office, London

HMSO (1988) *Report of the Inquiry into Child Abuse in Cleveland 1987* HMSO, London

Hoghughi, M., with Bhate, S. and Graham, F. (1997) *Working with Sexually Abusive Adolescents* Sage, London

Home Office (1968) *Children in Trouble, Cmnd 3601* HMSO, London

Home Office (1980), *Young Offenders, Cmnd 360* HMSO, London

Home Office (1984) *Cautioning by the Police: A Consultative Document* Home Office, London

Home Office (1985) *Home Office Circular 14/1985: The Cautioning of Offenders* Home Office, London

Home Office (1997) *No More Excuses: A New Approach to Tackling Youth Crime in England and Wales, Cmnd 3809* The Stationery Office, London

Home Office (1998a) *Criminal Statistics for England and Wales* Home Office, London

Home Office (1998b) *Draft Guidance on Establishing Youth Offending Teams* Circular 122/98 Task Force on Youth Justice, Home Office, London

Home Office (2000a) *Setting the Boundaries. Reforming the Law on Sex Offences* London, Home Office

Home Office (2000b) *The ASSET form* London, Youth Justice Board

Home Office (2001) *Criminal Statistics for England and Wales 2000* Cmnd 5312, Home Office, London

James, A. and Prout, A. (eds) (1997) *Constructing and Reconstructing Childhood, 2nd edition* Falmer Press, London

Jenks, C. (1996) *Childhood* Key Ideas Series, Routledge, London

Johnson, T. C. (1988) 'Child Perpetrators – Children who Molest other Children: Preliminary Findings' in *Child Abuse and Neglect* 12, p.219–229

Johnson, T. C. (1989) 'Female Child Perpetrators: Children who Molest Other Children' in *Child Abuse and Neglect* 13, p.571–585

Kahn, T. J. and Chambers, H. (1991) 'Assessing Reoffence Risk with Juvenile Sexual Offenders' in *Child Welfare* 70 (3), p.333–345

Katz, R. (1990) 'Psychosocial Adjustment in Adolescent Child Molesters' in *Child Abuse and Neglect* 14, p.567–575

Kelly, L. (1987) 'The Continuum of Sexual Violence' in Hanmer, J. and Maynard, M. (eds) *Women, Violence and Social Control* Macmillan, London

Kelly, L., Regan, L. and Burton, S. (1991) *An Exploratory Study of the Prevalence of Sexual Abuse in a Sample of 16 to 21 year olds* Child Abuse Studies Unit, Polytechnic of North London, London

Kelly, L., Burton, S. and Regan, L. (1992) ' "And what happened to him?": Policy on Sex Offenders from the Survivor's Perspective' in Prison Reform Trust (1992) *Beyond Containment: The Penal Response to Sex Offending* Prison Reform Trust, London

Kempe, C. H., Silverman, F. N., Steele, B. F., Droegemueller, W. and Silver, H. K. (1962) 'The Battered-child Syndrome' in *Journal of the American Medical Association* 181, p.17–24

Kilpatrick, A. (1992) *Long Range Effects of Child and Adolescent Sexual Experiences. Myths, Mores and Menaces* Lawrence Erlbaum Associates, New York

Kinsey, A. C., Pomeroy, W. B. and Martin, C. E. (1948) *Sexual Behaviour in the Human Male* Saunders, Philadelphia, PA

Kinsey, A. C., Pomeroy, W. B., Martin, C. E. and Gebhardt, A. (1953) *Sexual Behaviour in the Human Female* Saunders, Philadelphia, PA

Knight, R. and Prentky, R. (1990) Classifying Sexual Offenders: The Development and Corroboration of Taxonomic Models, in Marshall, W., Laws, R. and Barbaree, H. (eds) *Handbook of Sexual Assault* Plenum, New York

La Fontaine, J. (1991) *Bullying: The Child's View* ChildLine, London

Lane, S. (1997a) The Sexual Abuse Cycle, in Ryan, G. and Lane, S., (eds) *Juvenile Sexual Offending. Causes, Consequences and Corrections* 2nd edition, Jossey-Bass, San Francisco

Lane, S. (1997b) 'Assessment of Sexually Abusive Youth' in Ryan, G. and Lane, S. (eds) *Juvenile Sexual Offending. Causes, Consequences and Corrections* Jossey-Bass, San Francisco

Lane, S. with Lobanov-Rostovsky, C. (1997) 'Special Populations: Children, Females, the Developmentally Disabled, and Violent Youth' in Ryan, G. and Lane, S. *Juvenile Sexual Offending. Causes, Consequences and Corrections* 2nd edition, Jossey-Bass, San Francisco

Lane, S. and Zamora, P. (1982, 1984) cited in Lane, S. (1997) 'The Sexual Abuse Cycle' in Ryan, G. and Lane, S. (eds) *Juvenile Sexual Offending. Causes, Consequences and Corrections* 2nd edition, Jossey-Bass, San Francisco

Lanyon, R. (1986) 'Theory and Treatment in Child Molestation' in *Journal of Consulting and Clinical Psychology* 54, p.176–182

Littlechild, B. and Masson, H. (2002) 'Young People who have Sexually Abused. Law and Provision' in *ChildRight* July/August, p.16–18

Lovell, L. (2002) *I think I might need some more help with this problem* NSPCC, London

McGillivray, A. (ed) (1997) *Governing Childhood* Dartmouth, Aldershot

McLaughlin, E. and Muncie, J. (1993) 'Juvenile Delinquency' in Dallos, R. and McLaughlin, E. (eds) *Social Problems and the Family* Sage/Open University, London

MacKinnon, C. (1982) 'Feminism, Marxism, Method and the State: An Agenda for Theory' in *Signs* 7, p.515–544

Manocha, K. and Mezey, G. (1998) 'British Adolescents who Sexually Abuse: a Descriptive Study' in *The Journal of Forensic Psychiatry* 9 (3), p.588–608

Marshall, W. L. (1989) 'Invited Essay: Intimacy, Loneliness and Sexual Offenders' in *Behaviour Research and Therapy* 27, p.491–503

Martinson, F. (1997) 'Sexual Development in Infancy and Childhood' in Ryan, G. and Lane, S. (1997) *Juvenile Sexual Offending. Causes, Consequences and Corrections* 2nd edition, Jossey-Bass, San Fransisco

Masson, H. (1995a) 'Children and Adolescents who Sexually Abuse other Children: Responses to an Emerging Problem' in *Journal of Social Welfare and Family Law* 17 (3), p. 325–336

Masson, H. (1995b) 'Juvenile Sexual Abusers: A Challenge to Conventional Wisdom about Juvenile Offenders' in *Youth and Policy* 50, p.13–21

Masson, H. (1997) 'Researching Policy and Practice in Relation to Children and Young People who Sexually Abuse' in *Research, Policy and Planning* 15(3), p.8–16

Masson, H. (1997/1998) 'Issues in relation to children and young people who sexually abuse other children: a survey of practitioners' views' in *The Journal of Sexual Aggression* 3(2), p.101–118

Masson, H. and Morrison, T. (1999) 'Young Sexual Abusers: Conceptual Frameworks, Issues and Imperatives' in *Children and Society* 13, p.203–215

Masson, H. and O'Byrne, P. (1990) 'The Family Systems Approach: A Help or Hindrance?' in Violence Against Children Study Group, *Taking Child Abuse Seriously* Unwin Hyman, London

Masters, W. and Johnson, V. (1966) *Human Sexual Response* Little, Brown, Boston

Masters, W. and Johnson, V. (1970) *Human Sexual Inadequacy* Little, Brown, Boston

May, T (1993) *Social Research. Issues, Methods and Process* Buckingham, Open University

Meyer, J. (1996) 'Sexuality and Power' in *Theory and Psychology* 6 (1), p.93–119

Morrison, T. (4.6.1997), personal communication

Morrison, T. (2001) 'Surveying the Terrain: Current Issues in the Prevention and Management of Sexually Abusive Behaviour by Males' in *The Journal of Sexual Aggression* 7 (1), p. 19–39

Morrison, T. Erooga, M. and Beckett, R. (eds) (1994) *Sexual Offending Against Children: Assessment and Treatment of Male Abusers* Routledge, London

Morrison, T. and Print, B. (1995) *Adolescent Sexual Abusers: An overview* published by NOTA, Whiting and Birch, London

Muncie, J. (1999a) *Youth and Crime, A Critical Introduction* Sage, London

Muncie, J. (1999b) 'Institutionalised Intolerance: Youth Justice and the 1998 Crime and Disorder Act' in *Critical Social Policy* 19 (2), p.147–175

Nathan, S. (1995) *Boot Camps: Return of the Short, Sharp Shock* Prison Reform Trust, London

NCH (1992) *The Report of the Committee of Enquiry into Children and Young People who Sexually Abuse Other Children* NCH, London

Nellis, M. (1991) 'The Lost Days of Juvenile Justice?' in Carter, P., Jeffs, T. and Smith, M. (eds) *Social Work and Social Welfare Yearbook 3* Open University Press, Milton Keynes

Nelson, S. (1987) *Incest: Fact and Myth* Strathmullion, Edinburgh

North West 'Treatment Associates' (1988) in Salter, A. *Treating Child Sex Offenders and Victims – A Practical Guide* Sage, Beverley Hills

Noyes, P. (2000) 'Child Abusers Need Help' letter to *The Guardian* February 14th, p.19

O'Brien, M. (1989) *Sibling Incest* Safer Society Press, Brandon, VT

O'Callaghan, D. and Print, B. (1994) 'Adolescent Sexual Abusers: Research, Assessment and Treatment' in Morrison, T., Erooga, M. and Beckett, R. (eds) *Sexual Offending against Children: Assessment and Treatment of Male Abusers* Routledge, London

Olweus, D. (1978) *Aggression in Schools: Bullies and Whipping Boys* Hemisphere, Washington, DC

Olweus, D. (1993) *Bullying at School: What we Know and What we Can Do* Basil Blackwell, Oxford

Openshaw, D., Graves, R., Erickson, S., Lowry, M., Durso, D., Agee, L., Todd, S., Jones, K. and Scherzinger, J. (1993) 'Youthful Sexual Offenders: A Comprehensive bibliography of scholarly references, 1970-1992' in *Family Relations* 42, p.222–226

Parton, C. (1990) 'Women, Gender Oppression and Child Abuse' in The Violence Against Children Study Group *Taking Child Abuse Seriously* Unwin Hyman, London

Parton, N. (1985) *The Politics of Child Abuse* Macmillan, London

Parton, N. (1991) *Governing the Family* Macmillan, London

Payne, L. (1999) *Crime and Disorder Act 1998 Part 1: Background, NCB Highlight No. 171* National Children's Bureau, London

Payne, L. (2000a) *Crime and Disorder Act 1998 Part 2: NCB Highlight No. 172* National Children's Bureau, London

Payne, L. (2000b) *Crime and Disorder Act 1998 Part 3: NCB Highlight No. 173* National Children's Bureau, London

Pithers, W. and Gray, A. (1996) 'Utility of Relapse Prevention in Treatment in Sexual Abusers' in *Sexual Abuse: A Journal of Research and Treatment* 8(3), p.2–10

Pithers, W., Marques, J., Gibat, C. and Marlatt, A. (1983) 'Relapse Prevention with Sexual Aggressives' in Greer, J. and Stuart, I. (eds) *The Sexual Aggressor* Van Norstrand Reinhold, New York

Plummer, K. (1990) 'Understanding Childhood Sexualities' in *Journal of Homosexuality* 20, p.231–249

Pont, C. (undated) *London Boroughs and English Authorities Area Child Protection Committee Reports April 1990 – March 1992* DoH, London

Prentky, R., Knight, R., Sims-Knight, J., Straus, H., Rocous, E. and Cerce, D. (1989) 'Developmental Antecedents of Sexual Aggression' in *Development and Psychopathology* 1, p.153–169

Richards, J. (1990) *Sex, Dissidence and Damnation* Routledge, London

Richardson, G., Kelly, T., Bhate, S. and Graham, F. (1997) 'Group Differences in Abuser and Abuse Characteristics in a British Sample of Sexually Abusive Adolescents' in *Sexual Abuse, A Journal of Research and Treatment* 9, p.239–257

Ryan, G. (1999) 'Treatment of Sexually Abusive Youth: The Evolving Consensus' in *Journal of Interpersonal Violence* 14 (4), p.422–436

Ryan, G. and Lane, S. (eds) (1991) *Juvenile Sexual Offending. Causes, Consequences and Correction* Lexington Books, Lexington, Massachusetts/Toronto

Ryan, G. and Lane, S. (eds) (1997) *Juvenile Sexual Offending. Causes, Consequences and Corrections* 2nd edition, Jossey-Bass, San Fransisco

Ryan, G., Miyoshi, T., Metzner, J., Krugman, R. and Fryer, G. (1996) 'Trends in a National Sample of Sexually Abusive Youths' in *Journal of the American Academy of Child and Adolescent Psychiatry* 35, p.17–25

Sampson, A. (1994) *Acts of Abuse. Sex Offenders and the Criminal Justice System* Routledge, London

Scott, J (1990) *A Matter of Record: Documentary Sources in Social Research* Oxford, Polity Press/Blackwell

Seebohm Report (1968) *Report of the Committee on Local Authority and Allied Personal Social Services* Cmnd 3703, HMSO, London

Shipman, M (1981) *The Limitations of Social Research* 2nd edition, London, Longman

Smith, M. and Grocke, M. (1995) *Normal Family Sexuality and Sexual Knowledge in Children* Royal College of Psychiatrists, Gorkill Press, London

Sone, K. (1994) 'Man Enough?' in *Community Care* Inside Youth Crime, 28 July-3 August, p.4–5

Stermac, L. and Sheridan, P. (1993) 'The Developmentally Disabled Adolescent Sex Offender' in Barbaree, H. E., Marshall, W. L. and Hudson, S. M. (eds) *The Juvenile Sex Offender* Guildford Press, Guildford

Swenson, C., Henggeler, S., Schoenwald, S., Kaufman, K. and Randall, J. (1998) 'Changing the Social Ecologies of Adolescent Sexual Offenders: Implications of the Success of Multisystemic Therapy in Treating Serious Antisocial Behaviour in Adolescents' in *Child Maltreatment* 3 (4), p.330–338

The Bridge Child Care Development Service (2001) *Childhood Lost, Part 8 Case Review* London

Thorpe, D. H., Smith, D., Green, C. J. and Paley, J. H. (1980) *Out of Care: The Community Support of Juvenile Offenders* George Allen and Unwin, London

Trepper, T. and Barrett, M. (eds) (1986) *Treating Incest* Haworth Press, London

Tutt, N. (1999) 'Dealing with Young Offenders: A View at the Millennium' in *Community Care* 2- 8 December, p.i–viii

Varma, V. (ed) (1997) *Violence in Children and Adolescence* Jessica Kingsley, London

Wade, C. and Cirese, S. (1991) *Human Sexuality* Harcourt Brace Jovanovich, New York

Ward, E. (1984) *Father-Daughter Rape* The Women's Press, London

Wasserman, J. and Kappel, S. (1985) *Adolescent Sex Offenders in Vermont* Department of Health, Burlington, Vermont

Weihe, V. (1997) *Sibling Abuse. Hidden Physical, Emotional and Sexual Trauma* 2nd edition, Sage, London

Weinrott, M. (1996) *Juvenile Sexual Aggression: A Critical Review* Institute of Behavioural Science, University of Colorado, USA

Will, D. (1994) 'Impressions of the Tenth National Training Conference of the National Adolescent Perpetrator Network, Denver, Colorado, February 1994' in *NOTANews* June, p. 50–53

Will, D., Douglas, A. and Wood, C. (1994/1995) 'The Evolution of a Group Therapy Programme for Adolescent Perpetrators of Sexual Abusive Behaviour' in *The Journal of Sexual Aggression* 1(2), p.69–82

Wolf, S. (1984) *A Multifactor Model of Deviant Sexuality* Paper Presented at Third International Conference on Victimology, Lisbon, Portugal

Yates, A. (1982) 'Childhood Sexuality in the Psychiatric Textbook' in *The Journal of Psychiatric Education* 6 (4), p.217–226